the ULTIMATE
guide to
celebrating

Birth through Preschool

by
Linda LaTourelle

BLUE GRASS
PUBLISHING
Mayfield, KY

The ULTIMATE Guide to Celebrating Kids copyright © 2004 by Linda LaTourelle. ALL RIGHTS RESERVED. No part of this book may be reproduced or transmitted in any form by any means, electronic or mechanical, including photocopying and recording, or by any information storage and retrieval system, without the prior permission of the publisher.

For information write:
Blue Grass Publishing
PO Box 634
Mayfield, KY 42066 USA
service@theultimateword.com
www.theultimateword.com

ISBN: 0-9745339-4-7

1st ed.
Mayfield, KY : Blue Grass Pub., 2004

Blue Grass Publishers has made every effort to give proper ownership credit for all poems and quotes used within this book. In the event of a question arising from the use of a poem or quote, we regret any error made and will be pleased to make the necessary correction in future editions of this book. All scripture was taken from the King James Version of the Bible.

Cover Design: Todd Jones, Tennessee
LDJ Funky Fun font used with permission by Inspire Graphics
Proudly printed in the United States of America

First Edition © 2004

Thank You
(simple and sweet)

When the solution
is simple,
God is answering.
-Albert Einstein

Thank you... To each of you who have helped to bring

this awesome collection of sentiments to print. It is my prayer that the labor of love in this book will be far more reflected within it's pages, than my words in this simple note of thanks. These words of thanks are a mere symbol of my gratitude for your love, support and hard work in helping to share this dream with others.

Each of you who have helped know that it is my heart's desire to bring, to the reader, a book that will touch even one life and be treasured for a long time to come.

Thus said, it is with humble appreciation that I thank you. I am so blessed by this journey and the friends along the way. My life is ever growing through this endeavor, as well as the friendships, both old and new.

The greatest glory must go to my Lord, for He is my inspiration—in that He loved us so much.

May blessings abound to each of you...and may your lives be touched in as special a way as you have mine.

To my daughters, Dan, Todd, Shanda, Thena, Candy, Crystal, Paul, Camilla, my special ladies and their many prayers, my family and the endless list of inspirational geniuses that share in this work—THANK YOU!

My prayer would be that every one who reads this book would marvel at the incredible wonder of such an amazing blessing—a child. I believe to truly know and love a child is nothing less than a little bit of heaven brought down to earth and that each child is the ultimate echo of the heartbeat of God.

God Bless all of you...   —Linda

With deepest love and adoration,
I dedicate this book to
My Daughters...

I am so very honored to celebrate everyday with you. It is awesome experiencing how you have grown from enchanting, sweet babies into beautiful, exceptional and soulful young ladies. Words do little to express what I feel in my heart each day as I look at you. I am so very humbled knowing that God has blessed me with such an amazing love in you, my daughters.

It is with utmost love that I dedicate this book to you. God knew exactly my heart's desire when He called me to be your mother and I am so honored to share the ultimate love with you both. Please know that above all else (except the Lord) you are the joy of my heart, the light of my life and the very best of who I am or who I shall ever become.

I believe with all my heart, that if ever there were perfect love here on earth, I found it the day you both were born. Praise God for His awesome blessing—the two best girls in the world! I am honored to call you my daughters. Thank you so much for all your hard work, encouragement and most of all love for me. I pray that you will find a special blessing in this book and it will evoke fond memories.

May you always know how deeply you are loved and how special you really are—the best in every way, every day!

I love you

Momma

A child's love is the kind
that makes heaven touch earth
-Linda LaTourelle

Table of Contents

Table of Contents

Lucky is the woman who knows the wondrous joy of a child to love, for she has held the star of creation in her heart and heart of God in her hands.

—Linda LaTourelle

Let the celebration begin,
as it did so long ago...

I will praise you, for I am fearfully and wonderfully made;
marvelous are your works, and my soul knows very well.
Psalm 139:14

There is no greater miracle than the birth of a baby. As you read the pages of this book, may you reflect on the awesome gift of life . It is my hope that your life will be touched by every child you meet. Children are the future, and the love we give to them today will endure for generations.

Baby Love

For my beautiful daughters
the joy of my heart, the love of my life!

How Do I Love You?

How do I love you,
Let me count the ways.
I love you for this minute
And all the rest of my days.

I love you with our heart,
And know that it is true.
There is no greater joy,
Than the love I have for you.

I love you as a baby
And every day to come.
You are the greatest blessing
So awesome and such fun.

Forever I will love you
And hold you close to me.
For all you are is everything
A mother could ever need.

I love you with a love so grand
And treasure every day
When you reach out your little hand
We'll make memories and play.

For in His infinite wisdom
God brought our love together
A lifetime isn't long enough
Thank goodness we have forever.

-Linda LaTourelle ©2004

(Inspired by Elizabeth Barrett Browning)

The Wonder of It All

I stand in awe before
you, Lord
as I watch my child
at play.
How precious is
each action
And every word I
hear him say.

I know that as You
look down on us
we are so very small.

Yet, you know each
tiny grain of sand
And by name you know us all!

Lord, though my child seems small to me
As he stands upon your shore,
I know that were he ten feet tall
You could not love him more.

I cannot even fathom Lord,
How great your love must be
But I know that it is greater still
Than the vastness of your sea.

I stand in humble reverence Lord
As I watch my child in play
And know that you watch over me
In much the self same way!

And so I say a prayer of thanks
Dear Lord of earth and sea
For all the loving care you give
To both my child and me.
-Thena Smith © (See Bio)

Blessings come in many shapes, in sizes large and small, but a brand new little baby is the sweetest of them all

God's Gifts are the Best Gifts

Children Learn What They Live

If children live with criticism, they learn to condemn.
If children live with hostility, they learn to fight.
If children live with fear, they learn to be apprehensive.
If children live with pity, they learn to feel sorry for themselves.
If children live with ridicule, they learn to feel shy.
If children live with jealousy, they learn to feel envy.
If children live with shame, they learn to feel guilty.
If children live with encouragement, they learn confidence.
If children live with tolerance, they learn patience.
If children live with praise, they learn appreciation.
If children live with acceptance, they learn to love.
If children live with approval, they learn to like themselves.
If children live with recognition, they learn it is good to have a goal.
If children live with sharing, they learn generosity.
If children live with honesty, they learn truthfulness.
If children live with fairness, they learn justice.
If children live with kindness and consideration, they learn respect.
If children live with security, they learn to have faith in
themselves and those about them.
If children live with friendliness, they learn the world is a
nice place in which to live.   —Dorothy Law Nolte

I am so honored to include this wonderful poem in my
book. I have always believed strongly in the words of
this famous poem and have tried to live my life by example in how I raise my daughters. It is my passionate belief that every parent has the responsibility, to themselves
and the Lord above, to raise their child in an encourag-
ing, loving and nurturing environment.

Excerpted from the book CHILDREN LEARN WHAT THEY LIVE
Copyright © 1998 by Dorothy Law Nolte and Rachel Harris
The poem "Children Learn What They Live" on page vi
Copyright © 1972 by Dorothy Law Nolte
Used by permission of Workman Publishing Co., Inc., New York
All Rights Reserved

What Is Home Without A Baby

What is home without a baby,
With each gentle, winning way;
Sweet uplifted smiles inviting
Fond caresses all day?
Darling baby,
Precious baby,
Give her kisses all day.

Children

Stars to light our soul

The New Baby

There came to port last Sunday night
The sweetest little craft,
Without an inch of rigging on;
I looked, and looked, and laughed.
It seemed so curious that she
Should cross the unknown water,
And moor herself right in my room,
O my daughter, O my daughter!
Ring out, wild bells, and tamed ones too!
Ring out the lover's moon!
Ring in the little worsted socks!
Ring in the bib and spoon!
Ring in the milk and water!
Away with paper, pen, and ink,
My daughter, O my daughter!
-George W. Cable

Baby Land

How many miles to Baby-Land?
Any one can tell;
Up one flight,
To your right—
Please to ring the bell.
What can you see in Baby-Land?
Little folks in white,
Downy heads, Cradle beds,
Faces pure and bright.
What do they do in Baby-Land?
Dream and wake and play,
Laugh and crow,
Shout and grow;
Jolly times have they.
What do they say in Baby-land?
Why, the oddest things;
Might as well
Try to tell
What a birdie sings.
Who is the queen of Baby-Land?
Mother, kind and sweet:
And her love,
Born above,
Guides the little feet
-George Cooper

My mom says I'm her sugarplum.
My mom says I'm her lamb.
My mom says I'm completely perfect
Just the way I am.

Sometime you will know

Last night, my darling, as you slept
I thought I heard you sigh,
And to your little crib I crept,
To sing a lullaby;
Then bending low, I kissed your brow
For, Oh! I love you so
You are too young to know it now,
But in time you will know.

I am a precious masterpiece from God

A dreary place would be this earth
Were there no little people in it.
The song of life would lose its' mirth,
Were there no children to begin it.
-J G Whittier

Somebody said that it takes about six weeks to get back to normal after having a baby...somebody doesn't know that once you are a mother, "normal" is history.

- Our Little Blessing
- My Little Petunia
- Sweet Pea
- Rose Bud
- Sugar Pie
- Dumplin

- Baby Girl/Baby Boy
- Punkin'
- Little Man
- Dimple Dolly
- Pooh Baby
- Honey

A Baby is...

Sweet little cuddly bug with wiggly toes
A soft scent of powder and a tiny pink nose
Teddy bears, diapers and bottles galore
Giggles and grins with a smile to adore

Baby Loves Mama

Baby was "God's Masterpiece" since time and life began!

I count it as a privilege;
I count it cause for praise
To kiss my children goodnight
at the close of everyday.

A baby may grow too big for your arms, but never too big for your heart

Precious and priceless so loveable too, the world's sweetest miracle is a baby like you

If I never knew you
If I never felt this love,
I would have no inkling of
How precious life can be

When I held you, I found the missing part of me.

Blessed are the children

I think, at a child's birth, if a mother could ask a fairy godmother to endow it with the most useful gift, that gift should be curiosity. -Eleanor Roosevelt

- A Baby is Love
- A Baby is smile
- A Baby is snuggles
- A Baby is smart
- A Baby is thoughtful
- A Baby is giving
- A Baby is honoring
- A Baby is wonderful

Jesus Loves the Little Children

A child should always say what's true, and speak when he is spoken to, and behave mannerly at the table, at least as far as he is able. -Robert Louis Stephenson

The essence of God's
Wonder and Love
This is the gift
In our child from above

Children are Jewels
dropped from heaven

1/2 cup LOVE
1/4 cup KISSES & 1/4 cup hugs
Mix them together
And you get ME

Babies are the sweet peas in the garden of life

In the eyes of a child, love is spelled T-I-M-E

I'm spoiled, but not rotten!

A baby is a tiny piece of perfection.

If you think it is impossible to love someone more than yourself, have a child

It's not who wears the pants in the family who's boss, it's who wears the diapers.

If we are to reach real peace in this world we shall have to begin with the children. -Gandhi

With babies come laughter and love ever after

Googly-Goo

One small hand to hold in yours
One small face to smile
One wet kiss as he says "goodnight"
One small child forever more.

Catch a little love and put it in your heart
Save it for when you're old and gray
Baby is a darling, growing every night and day
Treasure every moment, count the many blessings
Love is in each second, thank the Lord and pray

Monday's child is fair of face
Tuesday's child is full of grace
Wednesday's child is full of woe
Thursday's child has far to go
Friday's child is loving and giving
Saturday's child works hard for its living
But the child that's born on the Sabbath
is fair and wise and good and gay

My mom says I'm a
super-special
wonderful terrific
little guy.
My mom just had
another baby.

Why?

A Star is Born

ONLY A BABY SMALL

Only a baby small,
Dropt from the skies
Only a laughing face,
Two sunny eyes;
Only two cherry lips,
One chubby toe;
Only two little hands,
Ten little toes.

Only a golden head,
Curly and soft;
Only a tongue that wags
Loudly and oft;
Only a little brain,
Empty of thought;
Only a little heart,
Troubled with naught.

Only a tender flower,
Sent us to rear;
Only a life to love
While we are here;
Only a baby small,
Never at rest;
Small, but how dear to us,
God knoweth best.
-Matthias Barr

Love
at first sight

THE BABY

Another little wave
Upon the sea of life;
Another soul to save
Amid its toil and strife.
Two more little feet
To walk the dusty road;
To choose where two
paths meet, the narrow
and the broad.

Two more little hands
To work for good or ill'
Two more little eyes,
Another little will.
Another heart to love,
Receiving love again;
And so the Baby came,
A thing of joy and pain.
-Mrs. Lucy E. Akerman

Baby's are a blessing from above
that fill our hearts with lots of love

You bet I'm cute

SOFT AS LOVE

A little form so dainty small,
So soft, so tender, and so dear;
A little voice whose helpless call
Is music to a mother's ear;
A little pulse of delicate breath
Like Eve's, when Zephyr whispereth;
A little arm that nerveless lies,
Red, curling fingers, tiniest things;
Two round, blue, upward-gazing eyes,
All filled with silent wonderings,
That, as the kiss of heaven's light bids,
Now ope, now close their downy lids.
A little head, so smooth and white,
Pert, rosy mouth and fairy chin,
And cheeks all rounded to the sight
Save where a dimple draws them in,
All in one tiny frame enwove,
As light as laughter, soft as love.
                              -W. Trego Webb

Born With A Silver Spoon

- Oh, so Cute!
- Ain't I Sweet!
- Babe In Arms
- Baby Of Mine
- Be My Baby
- Bundle Of Love
- Funny Face
- Gotta Love Me
- I'm Special
- Irresistible
- Its All In The Genes
- Little Darlin'
- Little Sweetheart
- Loverly Little Baby

A wee bit 'o Heaven

The Bottle Tree bloometh by night and by day!
Heigh-ho for Winkyway land!
And Bottle Tree fruit as I've heard people say
Makes bellies of Bottle Tree babies expand
And that is a trick I would fain understand!
Heigh-ho for a bottle to-day!
And heigh-ho for a bottle to-night
A bottle of milk that is creamy and white!
So cuddle me close, and cuddle me fast,
And cuddle me snug in my cradle away,
For I hunger and thirst for that precious repast
Heigh-ho for a bottle, I say!

God can never match the goodness
Of a trusting little face,
or a heart so full of laughter
Spreading sunshine every place.

A Baby Is...
Sweetness and delight
Everything that's right
Beautiful and precious, too
The very special part of you
She fills your heart with love
She's tenderness from above
-Linda LaTourelle

A tiny little
BABY
So innocent
and sweet
Will bring
love and
happiness
And make
your family
complete!
-Thena Smith ©

Baby Titles

- A baby is a bit of stardust blown from the hand of God
- A baby is teddy bears, rattles, powder and pins, meals at midnight, giggles and grins
- A baby is your baby forever & a day
- A baby is a touch of God's love
- A Boy is a Joy
- A Girl is a Pearl
- A Guardian Angel to Light the way
- A Honey of a Baby
- A hug a day keeps the meanies away
- Ah, those midnight snacks?
- All Wrapped Up!!
- Angel eyes
- Babies are a link between angels and man
- Babies are blessings sent from above
- Babies are bundles from Heaven
- Babies are life's most precious gifts
- Babies are little angels
- Babies are beautiful
- Babies are nature's way of showing people what the world looks like at 2:00 am
- Baby Love
- Babies are such a nice way to start people
- Babies are such sweet beginnings
- Babies fill a hole in your heart you never knew existed
- Babies touch the world with love
- Baby face, you've got the cutest little baby face
- Baby Philosophy: If it stinks, change it!
- Baby Steps

24

- Baby Talk/Baby Babble
- Baby, it's cold outside!
- Baby's sleeping I'm awake let's play!
- Bald is beautiful
- Bare Hugs
- Bear'ly One Years Old
- Bear-y Cute
- Beautiful Dream
- Bee Bop Babies
- Better check my diaper
- Birthday suit
- Blanket Baby
- Bonding for our first time
- Brat, who me?
- Bundle of Love
- Close to You
- Children are one third of our population and all of our future
- Close your little sleepy eyes
- Cootchie, cootchie, coo
- Cuddle bugs
- Cute as a Bug
- Cute as a Button
- Cute, but dangerous
- Cute? I invented the word
- Cutest Little Baby Face
- Daddy/Mommy's little girl/boy
- Daddy's Girl
- Diaper Duty
- Diapers by Gucci
- Did I say I was hungry?
- Discover Wildlife- Have Twins
- Don't know how! Never been trained!
- Don't let the diapers fool you; I'm the boss around here!
- Don't make me call Grandma
- Doo-Doo Happens
- Dreaming Sweet Baby Dreams
- Every life is precious
- Fairy tales do come true!

- Food Frenzy
- General Hospital
- Generation Gap
- Gift of Love
- Give me something good to eat!
- God Has Truly Blessed Us With Precious Gifts From Above
- Good Night Moon, Good Night Air, Good Night Noises Everywhere
- Got Milk?
- Growin' Like A Weed
- Growing Inch by Inch
- Hair's to You!
- Handle With Care
- In the swing of things
- Have you ever held a baby, a baby, a baby, a baby like this?
- He/she will fill our lives with sunshine and our hearts with love
- Help! Can anyone find the pacifier?
- Help! I've Fallen and Can't Get Up

- Helping Hands
- Here's a big Kiss
- Here I am—love me!
- Hold me, Feed me, Change me, Love me
- Hush-a-Bye Baby
- I am a Child of God
- I believe in angels!
- I wonder if these come in any other flavors? (Toes/fingers)
- I know I'm a handful
- If only she/he were sleeping instead of just recharging!
- I'm awake! Let's play!
- I'm Daddy's little tax deduction
- I'm Hungry!
- I'm just plane cute
- Baby, gotta love me!
- I'm Yours!

26

- I'm too sexy for my diaper
- In the beginning
- It's A Boy/Girl
- It's a "GRAND" world to behold
- It's hard raising parents!
- It's the Little Things in Life that Matter
- It's TOO quiet - where's the baby?
- Let the good times roll
- Little Bitty Pretty One
- Little boys/girls do cry
- Little Charmers
- Little darlin'
- Little Slugger
- Little Tax Deduction
- Look at that face
- Look how precious
- Look what's sprouting up
- Love in Bloom
- Magical Milestones
- Miles of Smiles
- Make room for _____
- March Showers Bring April Babies!
- Midnight giggles &grins
- Milk Does a Baby Good
- Miracle Baby
- Miss Rosy Cheeks
- Mommy, can we keep him/her?
- Mommy's Angel
- Mondays child is fair of face
- Moo Time
- More Milk Please!
- More precious than gold
- My Handsome baby boy!
- My name is NO NO NO, but grandma calls me precious
- My name is NOT No-No! It's oh how cute!
- Name that Food
- Nighty-Night
- Oh! Baby
- Once upon a lifetime
- Once upon a fairytale
- Once upon a Baby

- Once Upon A Time
- Once there was a precious little baby
- One Step For A Man Is One Giant Leap For A Kid
- One who sleeps with a blankie is comforted with love
- Our blessing from up above
- Our Little Cuddlebug
- Only One Like Me!
- Our gift from the Lord
- Our home has just been enlarged by 2 feet
- Our Little All Star
- Our Little Angel
- Our little love bug
- Our little sweetie
- Our littlest Angel
- Our New Arrival
- Our Rising Star
- Party in my crib—2 am
- Peek- a -Boo!
- People who say they sleep like a baby usually don't have one!
- Perfect 10
- Pose nude? You bet
- Practically Perfect in Every Way
- Precious Moments With Baby
- Precious Treasures
- Prince/Princess Pouty
- Queen of Cute
- Queen Cry Alot
- Rock-a-bye baby
- Saturday's child works hard for a living
- Sent from above
- Shake Rattle and Roll
- She/he will fill our lives with sunshine and our hearts with love
- She's somebody's baby
- Shhhhhhhhh
- Showers of Blessings
- Simple pleasures are life's greatest treasures
- So Big, So Sweet
- Somebody special
- Some sweet baby

⊛ Small/Tiny blessings make life a joy

⊛ So Cool, Just Gotta Wear Shades

⊛ So they sprinkled moon dust in your hair

⊛ Something wonderful has just sprouted

⊛ Special babies are the seeds in Gods miracle garden

⊛ Special Delivery

⊛ Spit Happens!

⊛ Sprung a leak

⊛ Star light, Star Bright

⊛ Straight from Heaven up above here is a Baby for us to Love

⊛ Sugar, Sugar

⊛ Sugar and Spice

⊛ Sweet Cheeks

⊛ Sweet Dreams

⊛ Sweetie Pie

⊛ Ten Tiny Fingers & Toes

⊛ Thank heaven for little girls/boys!

⊛ Thanks for the sunshine you've brought into my life

⊛ That's it! I'm going to Grandma's

⊛ The bare necessities

⊛ The Child born on the Sabbath day is bonny and blithe and good and gay

⊛ The Countess/Count of Cranky

⊛ The Duke/Duchess of Dirty Diapers

⊛ The Family Welcomes a New Star to their Galaxy of Love

⊛ The gift of love

⊛ The Journey Continues

⊛ The King of Cool

⊛ The little streaker

⊛ The Mammas & the Papas

⊛ The many faces of _____

⊛ The Most Precious Gift

⊛ The Pitter-Patter of Little Feet

⊛ The Little Prince

⊛ The Little Princess

⊛ The Princess of quite everything

⊛ The Story of my Life

- The One, The Only
- The prince/princess of Poutyville
- The Winner!
- The Young & the Restless
- Things that go "Bump" in the Night
- Time for a nap
- Tiny blessings make life a joy
- TOE-tally delicious!
- Toothless Beauty
- Tough Love is dirty diapers, messy eating and sleepless nights
- Udderly Adorable
- Waaaah!!!
- Watch out, here I grow
- Wet Baby Kisses
- What A Wonderful World
- What did they do before me?
- When do we eat?
- When I get big I'll get even
- Where is babies ear, eye, nose, mouth?
- Where's my hair?
- Who me?
- Who's that cutie?
- With A Face Like This, Life Will Be Smooth Sailing!
- With every little baby's birth, a bit of stardust falls to earth
- Yes sir, that's my baby
- You and me and baby makes three
- You are cut from a pattern I Love
- You Are the Sunshine of My Life
- You are the wind beneath my wings
- You bet I'm cute
- You Light Up My Life
- You're Daddy's Angel
- Yes Dear
- You're so precious to me cute as can be Baby of mine
- You've got the cutest little baby face
- Yum, Yum, Give me some!

When the Winds are Blowing

Roses red, and roses white,
Roses all a-glowing,
Nodding to my baby bright,
When the winds are blowing.

Little ships upon the sea,
Going, coming, coming,
One will sail to you and me
When the winds are blowing.

Little stars up in the sky,
Golden twinkles showing,
Clouds will hide them by and by,
When the winds are blowing.

Little ripples on the shore,
Inward ever flowing,
They will change to waves
that roar,
When the winds are blowing.

Little baby on my breast,
Sorrow all unknowing,
May God always guard your rest,
When the winds are blowing.
-Amy Blanchard ©

A cute little baby To cuddle and squeeze, to pamper and play with and bounce on your knees!

I know a baby, such a baby. Round blue eyes and cheeks of pink.

Oh, the bald head and oh, the sweet lips, and oh, the sleepy eyes that wink!

31

What Baby's Like

Baby grows like a flower,
Baby is fresh as a rose,
Daintily hued as the blossoms,
As the fragrant apple blows.

Baby is sweet as a song is,
The song of a twilight bird,
He's bright as the lark's gay trilling,
That early dawn has stirred.

Baby shines as a star does,
Gold gleams his darling head,
White pillow clouds around him,
Where he peeps out of bed.

Baby is dear as -- O, baby!
Nothing so dear can be,
In all the wide world's wonder,
As this little baby to me.

-Amy Blanchard ©

Sweet As A Song

Baby's Skies

Would you know the baby's skies?
Baby's skies are mother's eyes
Mother's eyes and smile together
Make the baby's pleasant weather.
Mother keep your eyes from tears
Keep your heart from foolish fears
Keep your lips from dull complaining
Lest the baby think it's raining.

Two tiny arms
To give you a hug
One tiny face
Cute as a bug
Cherry cheeks
And a button nose
Pretty in pink
And soft as a rose
-Linda LaTourelle ©

One tiny hand to
guide and hold
One tiny life to
shape and mold
Each little baby
is a gift from
God above
A symbol of his
strength and love

My baby kisses and is kissed,
For he's the very
thing for kisses.

Lucky is the
woman who knows
the pangs of child
birth, for she has
held the star of
creation in her
heart and heart of
God in her hands.
–Linda LaTourelle

BABY FACE

The nicest dreams that will ever be
Are the dreams shared by my baby and me
He smiles and clasps his tiny hand
With sunbeams over him gleaming
a world of baby fairyland he visits while he's dreaming
-Joseph Ashby Sterry

The Best Love of All

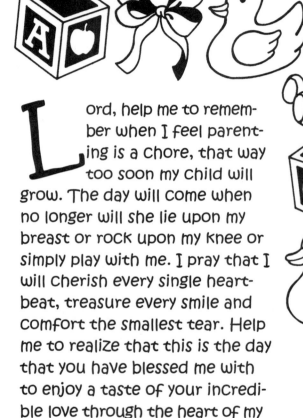

Lord, help me to remember when I feel parenting is a chore, that way too soon my child will grow. The day will come when no longer will she lie upon my breast or rock upon my knee or simply play with me. I pray that I will cherish every single heartbeat, treasure every smile and comfort the smallest tear. Help me to realize that this is the day that you have blessed me with to enjoy a taste of your incredible love through the heart of my child. How could anyone love me more than that?

-Linda LaTourelle

The Laughter of a child is the light of a house

'TiS the greatest gift
from heaven,
Little arms that
hold you tight,
And a kiss so soft and gentle
When you tuck them in at night.
A million precious questions
And each story often read,
Two eyes so bright and smiling,
And a darling tousled head.

Who is in that highchair
Keeping rhythm with a spoon?
Who has your full attention
Makes you crazy as a loon?

Who buys a baby
has to pay
A portion of the
bill each day;
He has to give his time and thought
Unto the little one he's bought
He has to stand a lot of pain
Inside his heart and not complain;
And pay with lonely days and sad
For all the happy hours he's had.
All this a baby costs, and yet
His smile is worth it all, you bet.
-Edgar Guest

Tweedle
Dum and
Tweedle
Dee
resolved
to have a
battle.
For
Tweedle
Dum said
Tweedle-
dee
Had
spoiled
his nice
new rattle.

A perfect example of minority
rule is a baby in the house

35

· · · · · · · · · · · · · · · · · · · ·

Babies are God's proof that the best things do come in small packages

Babies are nature's way of showing people what the world looks like at 2:00 a.m.

Bottles, rattles and cute little socks.

Lullabies, laughter &

alphabet blocks

- A baby is such a nice way to start a person
- A New Baby to Love
- A New Branch on the Family Tree
- A newborn's first thought, "Now what?"
- A Sneak Peek at Baby
- Momma's pride and joy
- B is for Baby
- Giggles and grins and dimples on chins
- A baby is a love that lasts a lifetime.
- If I have a monument in this world, it is my child
- Children are the keys to paradise
- A child is the heart of God
- Baby is Beautiful, Awesome, Blessing, Yours

Grow with him,
All your lives through
And he'll share a world
Full of joy with you.

36

One hundred years from now it will not matter what kind of house you lived in, or what kind of car you drove or how much money you had in the bank. But the world could be a better place because you were important in the life of a child.

The world shines bright with endless possibilities each time a child is born.

My SWEET

BABY

On the night you were born, every star, in every sky shone down in jealously, at the twinkle in your eye.
-Craig Castle

The angels light another star each time there is a birth to celebrate each precious child the good Lord sends to earth.

There is nothing sweeter than sleeping with your babies and feeling their breath on your cheeks.

It is not a slight thing when they who are so fresh from God, love us.
-Charles Dickens

LOVE

You crawled into our hearts long before you knew how.

You are our treasure.
You are our Angel.

BABY LOVE

One tiny hand to guide and hold,
One tiny life to shape and mold;
Each child, a gift from God above,
A symbol of His strength and love.

It's me, it's me! I'm here for you.

Baby Dear

Ten little fingers,
Ten little toes,
The sweetest of smiles
And a cute Little nose.

Happiness is having a baby to love, To cherish, to care for

Baby days are busy days
Of teddy bears and toys,
Of booties and bibs, rattles and cribs,
And the dearest kind of joy.

❀ A wee bit of heaven hear on earth
❀ A handful of happiness, a tummy full of baby
❀ Precious and priceless so loveable too.
❀ The worlds' sweetest miracle is a baby like you.

⚘ In the sheltered simplicity of the first days after a baby
is born, one sees again the magical closed circle, the
miraculous sense of two people existing only for each
other. -Anne Morrow Lindbergh

⚘ There was never a child so lovely as they slept in his
mother's arms

⚘ Having a child is surely the most beautifully irrational
act that two people in love can commit -Bill Cosby

⚘ There's no greater pleasure than a little baby to love
and treasure

⚘ A child is a beam of sunlight sent to warm our lives

A baby's feet, like sea shells pink,
Might tempt, should heaven see meet
An angel's lips to kiss, we think,
A baby's feet.
Like rose-hued sea flowers toward the heat
They stretch and spread and wink
Their ten soft buds that part and meet.
No flower bells that expand and shrink
Gleam half so heavenly sweet,
As shine on life's untrodden brink
A baby's feet.
-Algernon Charles Swinburne

Baby Dear, Our Baby Dear!
Praise the Lord we joyfully cheer
Beauty and love we see on your face
Touched so gentle by the Master's amazing grace
-LaTourelle ©

THE RACE

A little tear and a little smile
Set out to run a race;
We watched them closely all the while;
Their course was baby's face.
The little tear he got the start;
We really feared he'd win,
He ran so fast, and made a dart
Straight for her dimpled chin.
But somehow—it was very queer,
We watched them all the while—
The little, shining, fretful tear
Got beaten by the smile.

WEIGHING THE BABY

"How many pounds does the baby weigh
Baby who came but a month ago?
How many pounds, from the crowing curl
To the rosy point of the restless?

Grandfather ties the 'kerchief's know,
Tenderly guides the swinging weight,
And carefully over his glasses peers
To read the record, "Only eight."
-The Children's Book of Poetry

IN A GARDEN

Baby, flower of light
Sleep and see
Brighter dreams than we
Til good day shall smile away good night
-Algernon Charles Swinburne

BABY

if rhyme
be none.
for that
sweet
small
word
Baby.
The
sweetest
one ever
heard
-Algernon
Swinburne

Dance Little Baby

Dance, little Baby, dance up high!
Never mind, Baby, Mother is by.
Crow and caper, caper and crow,
There, little Baby, there you go!
Up to the ceiling, down to the ground,
Backwards and forwards, round and round;
Dance, little Baby and Mother will sing,
With the merry coral, ding, ding, ding!

SOFT KISSES

So new the kiss, so new the bliss
Of baby fingers tender—
A weight so warm upon the arm—
A sleepy breathing splendour!

And over thee, all warm, I see
Two tear-bright eyes bend softly;
And folded fast, upon thee cast
Are kisses falling softly.

Oh, tiny thing without a wing!
Oh, bird with song yet hidden!
Our guest, with glee we welcome thee,
To life's feast later bidden.

Dance Little Darlin'

Childhood—the enchantment of life!

Please help up Lord, we pray to Thee
With thankful heart, on bended knee,
To raise this child that he might be,
A happy child because of me -T. Greenfield

The angels from above, looked down and joy un-furled, as God so tenderly gave to us our little baby

From diapers and rattles
To mud pies and puppies
Dollies and teddies
To slumber parties all night
Party dresses and perfume
Oh how the years do fly
Now is the time for baby and I
I will treasure the memories always

A baby is a small member of the family that makes love stronger, days shorter, nights longer, the bankroll smaller, the home happier, clothes shabbier, the past forgotten and the future worth living for

- Star light, star bright, We jumped for joy at first sight

- Bottles, bibs, blankets and booties. Diapers, late nights and parental duties.

- Two little hands, two little feet, now our family is complete!

- Twinkle, twinkle little star. You are our awesome star.

- Star light, star bright, We fell in love at first sight

- The first steps a baby takes are into your heart!

- Oh my little Baby Dear, we're so happy now that you are here

For all the Laughter, smiles, and every tear, you'll Always be my Baby Dear

• • • • • • • • • • • • • • • •

Where did you come from, Baby dear?
Out of the everywhere into the here
Where did you get your eyes so blue?
Out of the sky as I came through
What makes the light in them sparkle and spin?
Some of the starry spikes left in
Where did you get that little tear?
I found it waiting when I got here
What makes your forehead so smooth and high?
A soft hand stroked it as I went by
What makes your cheek like a warm white rose?
Something better than anyone knows
Whence that three-cornered smile of bliss?
Three angels gave me at once a kiss
Where did you get that pearly ear?
God spoke, and it came out to hear
Where did you get those arms and hands?
Love made itself into hooks and bands
Feet, whence did you come, you darling things?
From the same box as the cherubs' wings
How did they all just come to be you?
God thought about me, and so I grew
But how did you come to us, you dear?
God thought of you, and so I am here
—George MacDonald

Itty Bitty Blessing

Two tiny arms to give you a hug
One tiny face cute as a bug
Cherry cheeks and a button nose
Pretty in pink and soft as a rose
-Linda LaTourelle

Little
hands will
grow so big
Tiny toes
will do a jig
Radiant
smile and
soulful
heart
You were
precious
from the
start

BAPTISM

Blessings on the little children,
Sweet and fresh from Heaven above,
May their days be filled with beauty,
May they grow in truth and love.
Lord, bless this tiny infant
Who will make the world so fair -
Keep this precious little life
Forever in Your care.

BLESS YOU

Bless you, my sweet miracle,
Angel of my heart!
Pure joy of life, too beautiful
To be a work of art!
In baptism
Such love of Him
May Christ to you impart.
-Nicholas Gordon © (See Bio)

JESUS LOVES ME

Rejoice & celebrate for you are a child of a King!

Oh, what a wonderful blessed day
I know God hears every prayer I pray
For here you are honoring the Father and Son
By being baptized, my little one!
-Thena Smith ©

The Family of God

With joy in my heart
I celebrate this day with you
and always will be here for you
wherever you are and whatever you do
-Thena Smith ©

Baptism or Confirmation

May joy and happiness fill your heart
And may this day set you apart
With honor to our God above
May you feel His presence and His love

-Thena Smith ©

On this day as you seek to grow
And more about your God to know
May you hear His voice
as He speaks to you
And to His commandments
always be true.

-Thena Smith ©

May you receive
His blessings
In such a way to
add unlimited joy
on this special day

-Thena Smith ©

God loves you

and cherishes you
for you are a treasure
His love for you exceeds
anything that can be measured

-Thena Smith ©

In my heart I have such joy
Over seeing the choice you made today
Such joy that could not be expressed
By any words that I might say
But I've stored in a very place
The awesome memories of this day
And be assured that for the rest of my life
They will be treasured and replayed

-Thena Smith ©

BAPTISM

Celebrate, celebrate
You are a babe in Christ!
May the fruit of the Spirit
Fill your life overflowing with joy!

This day is an answered prayer
that this moment in your life I could share.
May God bless you on this special day
and send Peace, love and joy your way.
-Thena Smith ©

Jesus loves me this I know
For the Bible tells me so
Little ones to Him belong
They are weak, but He is strong
Yes, Jesus loves me
Yes, Jesus loves me
The Bible tells me so

Christened for Christ

May God bless you
on this special
day and send peace,
love and joy your way.
-Thena Smith ©

The Story Begins

PERFECT TIMING

In this moment of your birth,
My heart soars, knowing that soon
My arms will embrace you
My eyes will at last gaze upon your beauty
My lips will whisper unwavering love to you, my child
In this moment I will treasure our very own miracle
And because of God's perfect timing,
You and I will bond eternally,
as mother and daughter
From this day forward, we will share
A love and a life together.
All that I have my darling daughter
is unconditionally yours.
I will hold this memory forever
In the deepest part of my soul
And from this blessed moment,
My life will never be the same
-Linda LaTourelle ©

Sweet Beginnings

You are more perfect than I could
have hoped for and more beautiful
than I could have dreamed.

Baby's Quiet Time

The clock on the nursery mantel
Softly strikes a melodious chime;
It's eight notes plainly telling
'Tis baby's quiet time.

As mama rocks her little one
She whispers a song of love
Cuddling so gentle and quiet
Blessed from heaven above
-Linda LaTourelle

A Mother's Joys

At evening, morning, every hour
I've an unchanging prayer,
That heaven would my babies bless
My hope, my joy, my care.
I've gear enough, I've gear enough,
I've bonnie babies three
Their welfare is a mine of wealth,

Baby, see the flowers! Baby sees fairer things than these, fairer though they be than dreams of ours.
-Algernon Swinburne

I do not love you differently, nor would I give up less. Of all that life has given me, to bring you happiness.

I have no name:
I am but two days old."
What shall I call thee?
"I am happy, Joy is my name."
Sweet joy befall thee!
Pretty joy!
Sweet joy but two days old,
Sweet joy I call thee:
Thou dost smile,
I sing the while,
Sweet joy befall thee!

OUR BABY

Tiny, precious slumbering babe,
Growing 'neath your Mother's heart;
You are the beginning of a dream,
We dreamed from the very start.

When we vowed before the Lord,
To become one as husband and wife;
We prayed for a special blessing,
Upon our children's lives.

How we dreamed of those children,
Now that day has finally come;
We see you sweetly growing there,
Our precious little one.

For you are now our heritage,
Our blessing from above;
A priceless part of our family,
A gift of our Father's love.

Allison Chambers Coxsey
©1995 (See Bio)

Simply Beautiful

- A Sneak Peek at Baby
- A Star Is Born
- Born to cause trouble
- Boy Meets World!
- Front page news
- Hello Little One
- Heaven Sent
- In the beginning
- Just arrived!
- Labor Day
- Now Appearing
- 'O Glorious Night
- Sent from above
- Today love has a name

49

Birth

- A brand new life
- A child is born
- A double blessing (twins birth)
- A time to be born
- A Whole New World
- A womb with a view
- And the Story Begins
- And then there was you
- Born innocent
- Born in the USA
- Doctor, Doctor give me the news
- Extra, extra...read all about it!
- Fasten your seatbelt, it's going to be a bumpy night
- First Edition
- Flowers bloomed on the day you were born
- God lent us an angel, sent from Heaven above
- Hip, hip hooray
- _____was born today

- I am a dream come true
- I loved you the first moment I saw you
- I'm here
- Joyous, the day you were born
- Labor of Love
- Little blessing from above
- Look what the stork brought
- Love at first sight
- Love is... a new addition to the family
- Make room for Baby
- Miracle Baby
- Miracle on 34th Street
- Miracles Do Happen
- New arrival
- On the day that you were born the angels got together
- Our dream came true

- ❀ Our new little star
- ❀ Presenting...
- ❀ Ready or not...here I come
- ❀ Special Delivery
- ❀ Stork Special
- ❀ Sweet beginnings
- ❀ Sweet Blessings From Above
- ❀ Sweet Mystery of Life
- ❀ Tell me about the day I was born
- ❀ The blessed event - Boy do I feel blessed
- ❀ The first time, ever I saw your face
- ❀ The miracle of life
- ❀ There is a great joy coming
- ❀ There's a kind of hush
- ❀ There will be showers of blessings!
- ❀ Today love came home
- ❀ Twinkle, twinkle, our little star, how we wonder what you are
- ❀ Welcome Little One
- ❀ We've only just begun
- ❀ When a child is born, the angels sing
- ❀ When they placed you in my arms you slipped into my heart
- ❀ What a miracle!
- ❀ What's all the fuss about?
- ❀ Yep, ten toes!
- ❀ You are my special angel

Little slight movements so catch my eye as you're floating there in your waterbed. A tiny rose fist opens up and gently waves, as emotions flood both my heart and head. Our child, such intense love I do feel for the tender moments first seen of you.
–Lottie Ann Knox © (See Bio)

Oh, the miracle of You

A child is born...

A precious new baby has come from above to live in your hearts and fill them

Baby Mine

JOY

A little child enters your life and fills a special place in your heart that you never knew

A baby is sunshine, moonbeams and so much more, brightening your world like never before.

A baby has a special way of adding joy in every single day.

A baby is a small member of the family that makes love stronger, days shorter, nights longer, the money less, the happiness more.

Simply Irresistible Sweetness

A small little child so precious and sweet has come into our lives to make them complete.

Believe in Miracles!

Birth

A child is the greatest gift
That our lives can bestow.
It brings the most exquisite joy
That we will ever know.
Some days deliver happiness,
Far more than we can touch.
We need the help of all our friends
To comprehend how much.
And so we thank you for the gifts,
Both those you brought and are,
That celebrate this rich, full life
And its rising star!
-Nicholas Gordon © (See Bio)

Celebrate

Before you were conceived we
wanted you. Before you were
born I loved you. And when
you finally came, it was nothing less than miraculous.

Miracles

The miracle of life is the most incredible experience one can have. It is so profound to realize that the infant in the womb will one day
become a living, breathing human being. What
an awesome blessing from above!

53

• • • • • • • • • • • • • • • • • • •

Pray Without Ceasing

You were the answer to my prayer
You were my dream come true
I asked the Father for a miracle
And He sent me you!

You were the greatest gift
That I could ever crave
I asked God for a precious gift
And you were the gift He gave!

You were the reason that I could smile
You were the words to the songs I sang
I asked God for for a tune
And He gave me everything!

He gave me a reason to wake up each day
With a baby to love and games to play!
He gave me a reason to laugh and to smile
Making my life seem more worthwhile!

The days were sweet when you were a baby
And grew sweeter every day
You brought me such joy and happiness
And brought unbounded love my way!

And each night when I count my blessings
I thank the Father above
For answering my yearning hearts deepest prayer
And sending you for me to love!
-Thena ©

God Answers Prayers

54

BABY GIRL
Nestled sweetly in your arms,
Is a touch of the Father's love.
A tiny, slumbering baby girl,

Fresh from Heaven above.
Cherish each tender moment,
As you look on her tiny face;
For you're holding a priceless treasure,
Wrapped in ribbons, roses and lace.

Soon, this tiny bundle of pink,
Will grow into a little girl;
With baby dolls and dress up clothes,
And a ballerina twirl.
With a sparkle in her laughing eyes,
She'll steal your heart away.
So hold tight to this special gift,
And memories of this day.
-Allison Coxsey © (See Bio)

Birth Day

We waited so long for this special day
For a child of our own to be sent our way

One little heart to love and adore
A child who is ours forever more

Birth Day
Happy birthday, dearest one,
Sweet child of my heart!
We've become one family,
Of which you are a part.
No more, no less my star!
We are one in love and joy,
In fondness and in worth,
And so as one we celebrate
This day, your day of birth!
-Nicholas Gordon © (See Bio)

Special Delivery

THE STORK

Last night the Stork came stalking,
And, Stork, beneath your wing
Lay, lapped in dreamless slumber,
The tiniest little thing!
From Babyland, our yonder
Beside a silver sea,
You brought a priceless treasure
As gift to mine and me!
Last night my dear one listened
And, wife, you knew the cry
The dear old Stork has sought our home
A many times gone by!
And in your gentle bosom

When a baby is born, so is a mother

I found the pretty thing
That from the realm out yonder
Our friend the Stork did bring.
Last night my heart grew fonder
O happy heart of mine,
Sing of the inspirations
That round my pathway shine!
And sing your sweetest long-song
To this dear nestling wee
The Stork from Way-Out-Yonder
Hath brought to mine and me!

Dream Baby

Last night a baby awakened upon her mother's breast. Oh, what a beautiful dream. My Baby, my little one know that I am blessed!

Babies are Hugs sent from heaven above

Pretty Baby

Hasn't any hair,
Just a ruff of gold down
Fit for ducks to wear
Merry winkling blue eyes
Noselet underneath
And a pair of plump lips
Innocent of teeth!
Either side each soft cheek
A jolly little ear
Painted like a conch shell
Isn't she a dear!

At cradle side sits Mother Goose herself,
the dear old mother,
and rocks and croons
In which the baby hearkens,
but no other her old-new tunes!
I think it must be so,
else why, years after,
Do we retrace and ring
with recollected laughter
Thoughts of that face,
seen yet unseen,
Beaming across the ages,
brimful of fun
and baffling all the sages
under the sun?

Sweet sugar Baby kisses

I Coo and Poo That's All I Do

57

Labor of Love

MAKES NO DIFFERENCE

Most new mothers as everyone knows
always count baby's fingers and toes.
And then much more often than not
She checks baby to see if it has got
Dad's shell ear shape and then again
maybe it is for his cleft in the chin.
She gazes at the round head shape
from silky soft hair on top down to nape.
She talks aloud as all mothers often do
to this tiny infant so innocent and new.
Thinking of names she leans toward dad,
this little treasure is best idea we ever had.
Makes no difference whether boy or girl
precious wonder, welcome to our world.
-Lottie Ann Knox © (See Bio)

CELEBRATING BIRTH

We celebrate the coming birth
Of an angel come to Earth,
Resembling now a basketball,
But soon our love, our life, our all.
-Nicholas Gordon © (See Bio)

The Wonder of Baby

What a change you have made in our life
When your first breath was drawn
The love of God shined upon us
And we tasted a little bit of heaven

● ● ● ● ● ● ● ● ● ● ● ● ● ● ● ● ● ●

EVERY CHILD IS A MIRACLE

It was a very special time, blessed by God above,
When a new live was formed out of my dear parent's love.
And every part of me was made with His infinite care...
From inside out He fashioned me before they were aware.
And soon my heart was beating, but still I was not whole,
Until God breathed into me, and gave to me my soul.
Created in His likeness, complete at last and free,
God performed another miracle—
When He created me!
Dorothea Barwick (C) 1995 (See Bio)

Lo, Children are a heritage of the LORD
Psalm 127:3

Blessings of love
Sent from above

The angels light another star
each time there is a birth
To celebrate each precious child
the good Lord sends to earth

The moment a child is born,
A mother is born, too

Blessed by Love

AMY MICHELLE

The little babe was crying, it wasn't out of fear
She didn't know to be afraid, she was so tiny there
Her nails were iridescent, her skin- soft as a rose
I looked upon that new-born face and felt my heart explode

Her lips were pursed, just like a bow; her eyes had such a healthy glow
The instant that I touched her hand, I knew one day she'd understand
I didn't make her heart beat, her blood was not my own
I didn't give her life, so sweet, I didn't make her bones

She came to me one cold December day
Her hazel eyes and soft brown hair were meant to be that way
Her body wasn't perfect, but God would see to that
It didn't matter anyway, I wouldn't give her back

Her tresses lay so softly curled upon her rosy cheeks
One day she'd know, a mother's love and, oh, the price is steep
It wasn't paid in dollars, it wasn't paid in cents
It was paid in love from up above and a bill was never sent

God sent an angel to me; He said "she's yours to keep"
I know she'll need a mom and dad to hold her tenderly
Some days she'll make you happy, some days she'll make you blue, but everyday will be a day to tell her, "I love you"   -Sandra Prouse (See Bio)

Announcing the arrival of the best little baby in the world
Born To Love

For I am fearfully and wonderfully made.

Psalm 139:14

You're invited to celebrate
This new life created in love

Baby's coming home
What a joyous day!

There is a little one on the way
So we're having a big party today

We're praising God
For his goodness and love
His perfect timing
Sent you here from above

We're jumping for joy
We're having a boy!

Baby is home
And all's well!

Baby dear is here
Come and see our doll

In our anticipation
Come join the celebration
Baby's coming
Won't you, too?

Peek-a-boo...what do you see?
A girl or boy? No, it's me!

We want to share the news
Our baby is coming in Twos

Whether a girl or boy, Babies are
special! Simple joy!

Baby's Coming Home

To rule the roost

A man never stands as tall as when he kneels to help a child. -Knights of Pythagoras

Pat a cake, Pat a cake, baker's man
Bake me a cake as fast as you can;
Pat it and prick it and mark is with a 'B',
And put it in the oven for baby and me.

Blessings come in many shapes, In sizes large and small, But a brand new little baby Is the sweetest of them all

Pat-a-cake, pat-a-cake,
Baker's man!
Bake me a cake
As fast as you can.
Pat it, and sift it
And throw it up high

If you're happy and you know it clap you hands
If you're happy and you know it clap your hands
If you're happy and you know it
then your face will surely show it
If you're happy and you know it clap your hands
If you're happy and you know it stomp your feet...

Adoption

PERFECT LOVE

Tonight as you lie sleeping
for the first time in your bed,
my heart is overflowing
with awe and amazement.

Born Of our hearts

You have become
our child
through the
grace of God
We love and
adore you.
What incredible
joy now that
You are home.
As we watch
your tiny face
We are so thank-
ful for you and
our blessings
overflow. The
wait is finally over and it's time
to begin to build our family.
We've prayed for so long
and now we understand
God's awesome timing
and His perfect plan.
You are the light of our life
The hope of our future
and the love in our hearts.
-Linda LaTourelle ©2004

Not flesh of
my flesh,
Nor bone of
my bone,
But none
the less, my
very own.

ADOPTION

Our family tree has been improved
Adoption made this so.
For love, much more than bloodlines,
Makes us thrive and grow.

JUST LOVE

Heredity or environment?
Which are you a product of?
Neither, my darling...neither,
Just two different kinds of love.

OUR CHILD

With anxious hearts and open arms,
we sought you everywhere.
You, dear child, are a gift from God,
The answer to our prayer.

FAMILY TREE

Our life and love we give to you
And all the joys to come
Our family tree is blossoming
With you our precious one.

FORMED BY LOVE

No matter whether birth or choice,
A home is blessed from above.
When caring parents claim their child,
A family is formed by love.

Never forget for a single minute
That you weren't born under my heart, but in it.

Motherless baby and baby less mother, brought together to love one another

Born not from our flesh, but born in our hearts, You were longed for and wanted and loved from the start. Conceived from a blessing sent straight from above

LABOR PAINS
The labor of my heart
The answer to my prayers
How long I waited for you
My love is ever true

Ｇod blesses us with precious gifts, but there is one beyond compare She's the sweetest little baby, an awesome answer to our fervent prayers

- Adoption Day
- Adoption Story
- A Gift From Above
- Birth Day
- Celebrate
- Getting Ready
- Getting to know you
- Hand-picked
- His Perfect Timing
- Labor of Love
- Love at First Sight
- Memorable Moments
- Our Family Begins

- Special Delivery
- The Hand of God
- Travel Journal
- Waiting is the hardest part
- Welcome Home
- With One Look at You
- Your new home

Ａ is for Adoption...
A wonderful way to start a family.
The answer to our prayer.
A gift of love so precious.
True joy beyond compare.

Tonight as you lie sleeping
For the first time in your bed
My heart is overflowing
With words that must be said
My love is brimming over
As I watch your precious face
Today my life is joyful because
Of God's wonderful grace.

- ❀ Our new little star
- ❀ Hand-picked with love
- ❀ Look what God did!
- ❀ Special Delivery
- ❀ Stork Special
- ❀ Sweet beginnings
- ❀ Sweet Blessings From Above
- ❀ God chose you for me
- ❀ Tell me about the day I was born
- ❀ My Forever Family
- ❀ The first time, ever I kissed your cheeks
- ❀ Born of my heart
- ❀ There is a great joy coming
- ❀ There's a kind of hush

- ❀ Today there will be showers of blessings!
- ❀ Today love came
- ❀ Welcome Little One
- ❀ Oh, Happy Day!
- ❀ When they placed you in my arms you slipped into my heart
- ❀ What a miracle!
- ❀ You are my special angel
- ❀ No pain-awesome gain
- ❀ The Perfect Plan
- ❀ Truly a gift from God

I prayed for this child, and the Lord has granted me what I asked of him -1 Samuel 1:27

For us to have each other is like a dream come true! We didn't give your life to you, but God knew what to do. He planned it out so long ago and knew just what you'd need. He found us longing for a baby that was sweet. Then in His perfect timing He opened all the doors to bring you home to us and bless our life with joy. –Linda LaTourelle

You are the labor of my prayers, the love within my heart. I prayed for you so desperately and cried so many tears. The child I longed to treasure seemed would never come my way. But in his perfect way God brought you home to me and every moment since that day is rich beyond compare. You are the greatest blessing that truly is so rare. Forever I'm your mommy and you my child so dear. No mother ever loved her child with a passion so deep. I thank my Lord each day and night for the love you give to me.
–Linda LaTourelle

Labor of Love Sweet gift from above God brought our darling babe home
-Linda LaTourelle

A is for Adoption

AMUSEMENT PARKS

- Fairy tales do come true
- A Pirate's Life for Me
- A Thrill a Minute
- Coaster Fanatics
- Feel the Magic
- Acting Goofy
- I don't wanna grow up
- Let the Adventure Begin
- Look, Ma, No Hands!
- Mad Hatter Tea Party
- Magical Moments
- Splash Down!
- The Happiest Place...
- The Thrill of it All
- Under the sea
- Ride the painted ponies
- Cotton Candy, Corn on the Cob & Cuddlin', Oh My!
- We're going down, don't throw up!

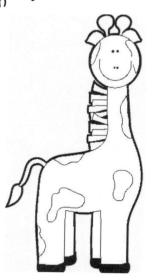

Wherever you go, what ever you do, May your guardian angel watch over you

Baby

Some say that angels have no wings
I know that this is true
For when I opened your baby blanket
There were no wings on you

A Guardian Angel
to Light the way
Keep Baby Safe
Night and Day

All night, all day,
Angels watching over me, my Lord
All night, all day,
Angels watching over me.

Babies are Angels that fly to the earth, their wings disappear at the time of their birth one look in their eyes and we're never the same They're part of us now and that part has a name

Sweet Baby
An angel from
the start,
A kiss blown
from heaven,
And caught by
my heart

Angel Baby

ART

PAINTED BLUE

I'm glad the sky is painted blue,
And the earth is painted green,
With such a lot of nice fresh air
All sandwiched in between.

- How fun thou art
- Artist in Training
- Imagine that
- Just a pigment of my imagination
- Little Michelangelo
- Look what I made
- Masterpiece
- Our little artist
- Our little masterpiece
- Painting to Perfection
- Sidewalk chalk art
- Sidewalk Picasso
- Magnificent Creation
- The magic paintbrush
- To imagine is everything
- You did it with flying colors

Laugh and play
Talk and sing
Teach him
stand by
his side
Dream
with him,
grow with
him,
all your
lives
through
And he'll
share a
world
full of
joy
with you
-MF Ames

70

ART

When you thought I wasn't looking I saw you hang my first painting on the refrigerator and I wanted to paint another one

- A Work Of Art
- Budding Artist
- Caution: Artist At Work
- Creativity Runs in the Family
- Cut and Paste
- He paints by the seat of his pants and his shirt and his hair.
- I'm not messy...I'm Creative
- Imagine That
- Look what I made!
- Our moody Monet
- Pint-size Picasso
- The Imagination Factory
- The Magic Paintbrush
- To Imagine is Everything
- What a Creation!

Every child reaches into his soul and paints his masterpiece simply to please himself

—Linda LaTourelle

All Children Are Artists

AWARDS

This is to certify that
(Child's Name)
has been a really great kid!
In honor of how helpful
and thoughtful you've been,
you are hereby presented with
the Little Angel Award.

The One, The Only
The Terrific
Awesome and Wonderful
Child of My Heart
(Child's Name)

You are hereby awarded the
Grand prize for being
Simply the Best
Kid in The World

FIRST PRIZE AWARD
(Child's Name)
Kid of the Year

- Outstanding
- Child of Gold
- Gold Medal Kid
- You're the Best
- Superior Student
- The Winners Circle
- Super, Stupendous
- My Super Star

- Beautiful, Bravo
- Incredible Kid
- Wow, Way to Go
- Winner of My Heart!
- Sensational, Special
- Magnificent, Marvelous
- Excellent, Exceptional
- I'm Proud of You Award

Bathtime Fun

BATH TIME

Once I'm in my bubble bath
I like to stir up more.
Half the suds go in my eyes
And half go on the floor.
The fun is in the bubbles 'cause
They giggle on my skin,
And when I stick them on my face
They dangle from my chin.
And when I splash them hard enough
They pop and disappear,
And then my bath time's over 'cause
I've made the water clear.

–Nicholas Gordon   2004 (See Bio)

Splish Splash I was taking a bath having a great time swimming like a fish then my fun was spoiled... Mom said I had to wash and get clean Nothing like burstin' my bubbles!

Bath

- A little dirt never hurt
- All Clean Now
- All Wet
- Bare bottoms welcome here
- Bath and Body Works
- Bath Time is Splash Time
- Bathing Beauty
- Bubble Baby
- Bubble Bath Fun
- Bubble Boy/Girl
- Bubble Fun
- Bubble your troubles away
- Clean as a Whistle
- Don't throw out the baby with the bath water
- God made dirt and dirt won't hurt
- Good Clean Fun
- Little Mermaid
- Making a big splash
- Pass the Rubber Ducky
- Private Bath, no peeking
- Rub-a-Dub Dub
- Rub-a-dub-dub, ___ kids in a tub!
- Rubber Ducky, You're the One
- Rubber Ducky, I Love You
- Scrub a Dub Dub
- Scrubbily bubbly
- Scrubby Dubby
- Splish, splash I was taking a bath
- Squeaky Clean
- Suds Up
- Tiny Bubbles
- Tub Time
- Tub Turtles
- Tubby Time
- Wash Day
- Wet n' Wild
- Where's my rubber ducky
- www.bathtub.com
- You make bath time lots of fun

At the Beach

What fairy-like music steals over the sea, entrancing our senses with charmed melody
-C. Wilson

By the sea, by the sea, by the beautiful sea...you and me, you and me, by the sea!

- A Day at the Beach
- A whale of a time
- Attack of the Crab Monsters
- Back to the beach
- Bathing Beauty
- Beach Baby
- Beach Ball Babes
- Beach Blanket Nap
- Beach Boy Baby
- Beach Bums
- Beauty on the Beach
- Bikini Brigade
- Baby by the Sea
- Castle Crashers
- Castles in the Sand
- Crabby Baby
- Down by the Bay
- Down By the Sea
- Fun in the sun
- Flipper Fun

Beach Baby

- Getting Their Feet Wet
- Hang Ten
- Happiness is... A Day at the Beach
- Happy as Clams
- Here Comes the Sun
- It Came from Beneath the Sand
- It Came from Beneath the Sea
- Itsy Bitsy Teeny Weeny Baby's Got a Cute Bikini
- Looney Dunes
- Making a Splash!
- Making Waves
- Mr. Sandman
- My First Bikini
- Ocean Fun
- On the Boardwalk
- Our Little Fish
- Our little Mermaid
- Paradise
- Peek-a-boo! I sea you!
- Poolside Pals
- Row, Row, Row Your Boat
- Sailing, sailing... over the ocean blue
- Sand castles
- Sand-Tastic
- Sea, sand and surf
- Seaside Treasures
- Sink or Swim
- Splashing' Good Time
- Splat!
- Belly Flopper

🪼 Splish Splash

🪼 Sun & Fun

🪼 Surf, Sand, Fun

🪼 Surfer Boy

🪼 Surfer Girl

🪼 Surfin' Safari

🪼 Swimmy Fun

🪼 Testing the Waters

🪼 That Sinking Feeling

🪼 The Jewel of the Pool

🪼 The Unsinkable

🪼 Treasures from the Sea

🪼 Under the Sea

🪼 Wave Reviews

🪼 We Love the Beach

🪼 Wet n' Wild

🪼 Whatever Floats Your Boat

🪼 You Rule the Pool

🪼 You're all wet

🪼 Down by the sea

Where the water is blue
I play in the sand
And romp and coo

By the sea, by the sea
With my baby and me
By the sea, by the sea
Oh, how happy we be
Baby and me by the sea

I'm swimmin' into my
Mommy's and Dad's heart

Building sand castles by
the sea, my baby and me

Row, row, row your boat
Gently down the stream
Merrily, merrily, merrily
Life is but a dream

Just mom and me
Down by the sea
Soaking up the sun
Having lots of fun

🏰 Our little pollywog

🏰 Born to scuba

🏰 Baby fish in the sea

🏰 Our little octopus

🏰 The "Star" Fish

🏰 Diving Diva

🏰 Scuba Dude

Birthdays

- _____ is One-derful!
- 2 is better than 1
- 2-rrific
- And a pinch to grow an inch
- Baby Takes the Cake
- Bearly one year old
- Birthday Bash
- Birthday Party Number One - I am having so much fun!
- Can I have another Birthday Tomorrow?
- Choo-Choo, __Turns 2
- Fantastic Four
- Fun being one
- Happy Bearth-Day
- Happy Birthday to You
- Have a Beary special day
- I wish for...

- It's fun to be one
- It's My Birthday
- It's my party and I'll cry if I want to!
- Just what I've always wanted
- Let Them Eat Cake
- Let's Party
- Look at me... I'm three
- Look Who's Two!
- Make a Wish
- M'm! m' Good
- It's the Big ONE
- One is Wonderful
- One year older and cuter too, Happy Birthday to you
- Party Animals
- Baby Birth Day
- Partytime Pretty

Birthday Blessings

- Party Down
- Party Girl
- Party 'til the cows come home
- Present Time
- Ready, Set, Blow
- So many candles... so little cake
- Surprise!
- Terrific twos
- That Takes the Cake
- The big One
- The more candle the bigger the wish
- There's no time like the Presents!
- They grow up so fast
- Three is Me
- Thrilling Three's
- The Star of the Show

- Time for Cake
- Today Is Your Day
- Triple Treat Today
- Two-rrific
- Under Wraps
- We need more candles
- We're havin' some fun now
- Where's the Party?
- You can't have your cake and eat it too
- You can't wear your cake and eat it too
- You take the Cake!

Body Beautiful

BABY SKIES

Would you know the baby skies?
Baby's skies are mother's eyes.
Mother's eyes and smile together
Make the baby's pleasant weather.

Mother, keep your eyes from tears,
Keep your heart from foolish fears,
Keep your lips from dull complaining
Lest the baby think 'tis raining.

-Mary C. Bartlett

BUTTON NOSE

She had a button nose, and curls upon her head
This tiny little fairy, that slept beside my bed
I never saw her in the day, but silently at night
I'd find her on my bedroom floor, wrapped in a blanket tight

Sometimes she would wake me with her giggles of delight
And then she'd flash a smile at me in the soft moon light
Her eyes were bright and shiny, her fingers soft and smooth
And sometimes she lay next to me, when she was in the mood

I don't know where she came from, I don't know where she went
But often in my dreams at night, she stands beside my bed
Her face is always smiling, I know that she's my friend
Perhaps one day she will return and I'll see her once again
- Sandra Prouse © (See Bio)

BABY FACE

You've got the cutest little baby face
No one could ever take your place
Your smile is like a ray of sun
You are my precious little one

What would you take for that soft little head
Pressed close to your face at time for bed
With a white, dimpled hand in your own held tight,
And the dear little eyelids
Kissed down for the night?
What would you take?

What would you take for that smile in the morn,
Those bright, dancing eyes and the face they adorn:
For the sweet little voice that you hear all the day
Laughing and cooing-yet nothing to say?

What would you take for those cute little feet,
Cheeks so rosy and kisses so sweet
Nothing I say
Can replace the love
God gave a gift
so blessed from above
So if you are asking how much I would take
No love would a mother begin to forsake.

Eyes of blue
Eyes of brown
Eyes of love
Sleep so sound

Sophisticated, worldly-wise, I searched for truth and found it not. And then one day, when the world forgot, I found it right there in my baby's eyes.

Some say my smile is like Daddy's
Some say my eyes are like Mommy's
But most of all, I hope they say
My heart is like Jesus'

Blessings come in many shapes from bigger down to small, but a new little baby is the sweetest blessing of all.

Curly Top

Growing Up

I kicked and stretched and wiggled,
'Twas surprising how I grew.
Each day that I got bigger,
I got better looking, too!

In blue flame of color
Asters fun wild,
And blue innocently
blue, are the eyes of
a child.
-Katherine Edelman

Sweet Cheeks

What would you take for that smile in the morn,
Those bright, dancing eyes and the face they adorn:
For the sweet little voice that you hear all day

Baby

days are busy days of teddy bears and toys, of booties and bibs, rattles and cribs and the dearest kind of joys

- Twinkle Little Toes
- Pinky Petunia
- Ebony Eyes
- Baby Blues
- Tiny Toes
- Kissy Face
- Bed Head
- Wild and Wooly
- Little Miss America
- Glamour girl
- Gorgeous and Girlie
- Beautiful Babe
- Fair Maiden
- Sir Love-a-lot
- Prince Kissy Face
- Love that Face
- Born Beautiful
- Breathless
- Baby Blue Eyes
- Brown Eyed Girl
- Look at that Face
- Cherry Cheeks
- Delightful Dimples
- What a Doll!
- 100% Adorable

- American Beauty
- Baubles and Bangles
- Beauty & the Beast
- Call Me Irresistible
- Color Me Beautiful
- Dressing Up
- Feelin' Frilly
- I Feel Pretty
- Pretty Princess
- Pretty Baby
- Ooh La-La!
- Sitting Pretty
- Picture Perfect
- Perfection
- Isn't She Lovely?
- I Enjoy Being a Girl
- Can't take my eyes off from you
- Mirror, mirror what's the word?

A face only a mother can love

Jesus, See A Little Child

Jesus, see a little child,
Kneeling at its mother's knee;
Meekly pleading at thy feet,
Lifting up its hands to Thee.
Savior, guide my little steps,
Never let them halt or stray;
Wash me with Thy precious blood;
Jesus, take my sins away!

Make me gently, make me good,
Let no evil fill my heart;
Never leave me night or day,
Watch me when I play or rest.
Jesus, Savior of the world,
Look with pity down on me;
Though I'm but a little child,
Teach me how to pray to Thee!
-Matthias Barr

In A Garden

Baby, see the flowers!
—Baby sees fairer than these,
Fairer though they be than dreams of ours.
Baby, hear the birds!
—Baby knows
Better songs than those,
Sweeter though they sound than sweetest words.
Baby, see the moon!
—Baby's eyes
Laugh to watch it rise,
Answering light with love and night with noon.

I have two eyes to see with,
I have two feet to run,
I have two hands to wave with,
And nose I have but one.
I have two ears to hear with,
And a tongue to say "Good day".

Million $ Smile

Dimple Darling Daddy's Delight

Perfection

You are more perfect than I could have hoped,
more beautiful than I could have dreamed,
more precious than I could have imagined
I love you more than I could have known

Chin Chopper

Here sits the Lord Mayor,
Here sit his two men,
Here sits the cock,
Here sits the hen,
Here sit the little chickens,
Chin-chopper, chin-chopper, chin!

Head and shoulders,
knees and toes.
Knees and toes, knees
and toes
Head and shoulders,
knees and toes
Make your feet go
stamp, stamp, stamp.

Nose and elbows, feet
and waist
Feet and waist, feet
and waist
Nose and elbows, feet
and waist
Make your hands go
clap, clap, clap.

Boo Boo's

- A pound of cure
- A stitch in time
- A time to heal
- Against all odds
- Break it to me gently
- Bumps and bruises
- Give me a break
- On the mend
- Oops!
- Ouch
- Stitch by stitch
- The healing touch
- Them's the breaks
- This too shall pass
- Time heals all wounds

- Mommy Kiss It?
- Make it Better
- Boo-Boo Time
- Owie Wowie
- Waaaaaaaa...
- Kiss the hurt away
- Sign my Cast
- Mommy it hurts
- Scratches & Scrapes
- Big Shiner

Baby's Black-eye

Today I had a crash
It happened in my bed
I took a big ole' tumble
And hit my baby head!
I banged my eye and head
But that's not the only part
The pain went right through me,
Into my mommy's heart!
-Thena Smith ©

Band-aid

When I fall and scrape my knee
My mommy puts a band-aid on me!
Knee or leg or face or chin
My mommy puts a band-aid on them!
If I have a tummy ache
In the middle of the night
Mommy comes into my room
Even if there is no light!
She brings me stuff to make it stop
The hurting that I feel inside
And she knows that I feel better
After I have cried.
If I have a bad day at school
And I just need to talk.
My mommy gets her sweater on
And we go for a walk.
When I have had a awful day
Or hurt myself while I played
My Mommy and her hugs and kisses
Are better than the best bandaid!
-Thena ©

My Knees

Sometimes during a fun day
I scrape my knees while I'm at play
Even when they're black and blue
My mom knows just what to do.

Sometimes if I've fallen really hard
A dose of medicine might be required
But usually it's just a scratch I've taken
And my body is just a wee bit shaken.

When Mom comes and cleans up my knee
She gives a hug and kiss to me.
I don't mind the kiss at all--
It's kind of nice when you've had a fall!
-Thena Smith ©

Boogers

The Boogie Song

Oh sing me a song about boogies
You know I can pick them with style
If it came to a national championship
I'd win by a good country mile

With my finger stuck well up my nostril
I'd pick 'till the boogie was free
Then it's up to the light for inspection
Before gobbling it down with great glee

So I hope that my parents are listening
And give all the moaning a rest
You can keep all your pasta, roast beef and peas
Because I like boogies the best
-Rob Erskine © (See Bio)

Boys

Only God Could Create a Little Boy

Look at that wonderful creature
That we call a little boy
Only God in Heaven above
Could create such a package of joy!

Who would have thought of all of the things
That occupy a little boys mind?
If we were to look inside his head
What wonderful things would we find?

His imagination when let run free
Lets him wondrous things to see
And he finds joy in all manner of things
From rocket ships to tennis shoestrings!

He can love a puppy dog or a rat
With just as much ease
And when given the opportunity
A little boy loves to please.

Human beings can create
All manner of things
to bring joy
But only a wonderful
God of love
Could have created
a little boy!
Thena Smith ©

90

Baby Boy

All the dreams you ever dreamed,
About a baby boy;
Are wrapped up in this bun-
dle of blue,
Who gives you so much joy.
So quickly he will start to grow,
And time will fly so fast.
Just hold tight to his little hand,
And make each moment last.
For soon he'll be a little boy,
With busy hands and dirty face;
Frogs & marbles & puppies in tow,
Running from place to place.
Right now he's fresh from Heaven,
A gift for you to love.
A tiny, sleeping, bundle of blue,
Sent from the Father above.
Allison Chambers Coxsey © (See Bio)

There is nothing like the blessing Of a bouncing, baby boy He will fill your home with energy And touch your heart with joy. He'll hug you and bug you and try you within But each precious memory you'll treasure again and again. —Linda LaTourelle

☆ A boy is a magical creature--you can lock him out of your workshop, but you can't lock him out of your heart. -Allan Beck

☆ A man can never quite understand a boy, even when he has been a boy. -Chesterton

☆ Boys are beyond the range of anybody's sure understanding, at least when they are between the ages of 18 months and 90 years. -James Thurber

☆ Boys will be boys, and so will a lot of middle-aged men. -Kin Hubbard

☆ Life's filled with wonder and always a joy, When you share life with your little boy.

☆ No earthly joys could bring more pleasure than little boys to love and treasure.

☆ Of all the animals, the boy is the most unmanageable. (Plato)

☆ Of all the blessings God sends from above, the one most precious is a baby boy to love.

☆ One small hand to hold in his One small face to smile. One small kiss and she says good-night One small child

☆ Popsicle kisses and big bear hugs, Little boy trains and jars full of bugs.

☆ Snips and snails and puppy dogs tails; that what little boys are made of.

☀ The glory of the nation rests in the character of her men. And character comes from boyhood. Thus every boy is a challenge to his elders. -H. Hoover

☀ The night you were born I ceased being my father's boy and became my son's father. That night I began a new life.

☀ There is nothing so aggravating as a fresh boy who is too old to ignore and too young to kick. -Kin Hubbard

☀ Trust with dirt on its face, Beauty with a cut on its finger, Wisdom with bubble gum in its hair, and the Hope of the future with a frog in its pocket.

All American Boy

When you can't do anything else to a boy, you give a boy enough rope and he'll bring home a stray dog on the end of it.

LITTLE BOYS

Dirty little faces, patches on his knees
Marbles in his pockets, climbing up some trees
Little boys are curious in many different ways
Like how to fix a bike or fish on summer days
He can't resist a puddle after a morning rain and
dreams of far off places watching a passing train
He is daddy's helper with a hammer and some nails
He has a love for creepy things and anything with tails
Collecting is a past time which little boys love to do,
from baseball cards to bottle caps and some ball
caps to among his many treasures that he stores be-
neath his bed old comic books, a street sign and
something he named Fred.
Little boys are warriors fighting Ninja style
And pepperoni pizza is sure to win a smile
He hides his sister's dolly just to hear her cry
But, he will defend her if trouble passes by
Little boys are made of mischief, energy and love
They are sure to bring a chuckle to our Lord above
The greatest gift of heaven comes bundled in baby
blue when he gives a hug and kiss saying,
"Mommy I love you,"
-Barbara K. Cox

- 100% Boy
- A boy is . . .
- All American Boy
- All Boy
- Bouncing Baby Boy
- Boy Meets World!
- Boys and their toys
- Boys Will be Boys
- Boys-n-Toys
- Boys'R'us
- Daddy's little boy
- Daddy's Little Helper
- First set of wheels
- Genuine Boy
- Howdy, L'il Buckaroo!
- If I had a hammer...
- I'm a Big Boy Now
- It's a Boy!
- It's a Guy Thing
- I've been working on the railroad
- Just Like Dad
- Just me & my Pa
- Just one of the guys
- Like Father, Like Son
- Little Bit
- Little Boy Blue
- Little boys are angels too!
- Little boys are treasures
- Little boys do cry
- Little slugger
- Men At Work
- Mommy's "Son" flower
- Mommy's little boy
- My _____ Sons
- So handsome!
- Thank God I'm a Country Boy
- Thank Heaven for Little Boys
- The Boy from New York City
- The Son Also Rises
- Tool Time
- Tough as nails
- Wonder Boy
- You Are My Son-shine

BUBBLES

Blowing Bubbles

Dip your pipe and gently blow.
Watch the tiny bubble grow
Big and bigger, round and fat,
Rainbow colored and then-
SPLAT!
-Margaret Hillert

Big bubbles
Little bubbles
Fat and round
So many bubbles
To be found
Can you pop
them
One by one
popping bubbles
All day long

- Bubble Baby
- Bubble Bash
- Bubble Bath Fun
- Tiny Bubbles
- Bubble Boy/Girl
- Bubble Bobble
- Bubbly, bubbles
- Bubble Fun
- Bubble your
  troubles away

POP! Bubbles
in the
bath and
bubbles on your head
How about *some* bubbles
on your body, instead?

BUGS AND MORE

FIRE FLIES

See the air filling near by and afar,
A shadowy host—how brilliant they are!
Silently flitting, spark upon spark,
Gemming the willows out in the dark;
Waking the night in a twinkling surprise,
Making the star-light pale where they rise; *Bzzz...*
Startling the darkness, over and over,
Where the sly pimpernel kisses on the clover;
Piercing the duskiest heights of the pines;
Drowsily poised on the low-swinging vines;
Suddenly shifting their tapers around,
Now on the fences, and now on the ground,
Now in the bushes and tree-tops, and then
Pitching them far into darkness again;
There like a shooting-star, slowly on wing,
Here like the flash of a dowager's ring;
Setting the dark, croaking hallows a-gleam,
Spangling the gloom of the ghoul-haunted stream;
They pulse and they sparkle in shadowy play,
Like a night fallen down with its stars all astray;
They pulse and they flicker, they kindle afar,
A vanishing hose,--but how brilliant they are!
-Mary Mapes Dodge

TO A BEE

Busy Bee, busy Bee, where are you going?
Down where the blue-bells are bud-
ding and blowing, There I shall find
something hidden and sweet
That all little children are willing to eat!
Busy, Bee, busy Bee, what will you do?
Put it into my pocket, and save it for you!
-Maud Keary

FIREFLIES

Flickering lights flit through the night
The breeze is soft and warm
Fairies dancing in the dark
Catching fireflies in a jar
Games of hide and seek are played
As the fairies gaily dance and sway
Behind a bush or under a flower
A fairy found with a fireflies power
A thousand wings shed golden light
Like tiny light bulbs in the night
Dots of light that glow and dim
As they're carried merrily on a fairy's whim

-Sandra Prouse

Oh, Bugs!

FIREFLY LIGHT

Now in the summer
Dew and damp,
The firefly lights
His little lamp.
I'm sure his lamp's
Clear flickering light
Is like a beacon
In the night
For creepy, crawly
Creatures who
Might lose their way
In damp and Dew

- A bug's life
- Antics
- Are free
- Be my luv bug
- Bee good
- Bee happy
- Bee joyful
- Bee kind
- Bee mine
- Bee sweet
- Bee tender
- Bee wise
- Bee-u-ti-ful butterfly!

- Baby Bug
- Bedbug
- Beeyond
- Bug colletin'
- Bug hunting
- Bug swarm
- Bugging out
- Busy as a bee
- Butterflies
- Butterfly kisses
- Buzzzzzzz
- Buzzy as a Bee
- Cuddle bugs
- Cute as a bug in a rug
- Digging for worms
- Don't bug me
- Earth worms
- Here's the buzz
- Honey of a day
- Honey, I love my kids
- Itsy bitsy Spider
- Ladybug Baby
- Lice ain't nice
- Lovely little bug
- Mad as a hornet
- My "bee-utiful" kids

- Our bee-utiful baby
- Our bee-utiful child
- Our little love bug!
- Pocketful of worms
- Snug as a bug in a rug
- Snuggle bugs
- Social butterflies
- Some Honey loves you
- Sometimes you're the windshield, sometimes you're the bug
- The antz go marching one by one....
- The buzz
- The flu bug
- The latest buzz
- The Queen Bee
- Un"bee"lievable cute
- Waterbugs
- We bee-lieve in love
- You're my honey bee

BUT WHY?

WHY?

Why does the tide go in and out?
Or the moon is seen at noon?
And why does Dad, when I ask him when
Always tells me, "Soon"
Why do snowmen melt so fast
But take so long to make?
And why does Mum say, "Off to bed"
When I am wide awake?
Why does my toast fall butter down
When it falls from off my plate?
And why do all the spiders
Weave their webs on my front gate?
Why does the sun, before it sleeps
Change from gold to red?
And why have I not seen the mouse
That lives in my Dad's shed?
Why do I ask so many things
You ask me with a sigh
I want to learn about my world
'Cause I'm curious, that's WHY!
☺
Mommy how do birds fly?
Mommy why do babies cry?
Mommy why do flowers smell?
Mommy how'd the snail get a shell?
Mommy why do you know everything?
Mommy you just make my heart to sing.

I LOVE YOU

LITTLE GIRLS QUESTIONS

Whose bonny blue bowl is the sky, Mamma,
So shining, so round, and so deep?
The angles, perhaps, come down there to drink,
Do you think,
When baby & I are asleep?
The stars,—are they lamps set thick in the blue,
To brighten the beautiful home?
To light them and hang them,
who climbs so high
To the sky?
Baby and I never see him come.
Are the clouds white beds in the sky, Mamma,
Piled snowy and soft and so high,
Way up in the highest sky?
Do they sleep far up there,
as sweetly and warm,
Safe from harm,
As you and the baby and I?
The moon, I am sure, is a golden boat,—
Who sails in it, softly, to-night?
Some angel, you think, all loving and fair,
That takes care
Of baby and me, till the light?
The dark is a curtain, so warm and so close;
God drops it all round us at eve;
At light, when it lifts, if we wake, maybe
We can see—
The Baby and I—Into Heaven!!

CANDY

If...
The rivers were made of jelly
The roads were paved with chocolate
The sun was a giant orange
The ocean was full of punch
The sand was colorful sprinkles
The rain was gumdrops
The snowflakes were coconut
The moon was marshmallow fluff
The houses were built of gingerbread
The cars all hard rock candy
The flowers were lollipops
The grass was licorice sticks
Then...
Everyday would be so sweet
And life would always be great to eat.

Sweet Sugar Babe

I'm Mommy's cutie pie
The apple of Daddy's eye
I'm kisses and hugs
And a Sweetie Bug
I guess that's why
They call me Sugar!

You're my sugar pie
Honey bunch
Yummy gummy gum drop
Lollipop, cupcake
Taffy twists and cherries
Sweetness and light
So very good

Scripture reading is lots of fun...
'Specially while chewing bubble gum!
Read the scriptures while you chew,
And when the flavor's gone...
You're through

Jelly Beans For Jesus

Red is for the blood He gave.
Green is for the grass He made.
Yellow is for the sun so bright.
Orange is for the edge of night.
Black is for the sins that were made.
White is for the grace He gave.
Purple is for the hour of sorrow.
Pink is for the new tomorrow.

I Love You

I love you, I love you
I love you divine
Please give me
your bubblegum
You're sitting on mine!

Sweet on Jesus

Does your
Chewing gum
Lose it's flavor
On the bedpost
Overnight?

- ✤ Cookie Crumbs
- ✤ Cookie Monster
- ✤ Here's the Scoop
- ✤ How Sweet It Is
- ✤ Jam Session
- ✤ Life is Sweet
- ✤ Sugar Shock
- ✤ Sugar Sugar

- ✤ Sweet Beginnings
- ✤ Sweets for the Sweet
- ✤ You Take the Cake
- ✤ Peanut butter and belly
- ✤ The Candyland Kids
- ✤ Caught With a Hand in the Cookie Jar
- ✤ Hand over the Chocolate and No One Gets Hurt

CASTLES

THE CASTLE-BUILDER

A gentle boy, with soft and silken locks,
A dreamy boy, with brown and tender eyes,
A castle-builder, with his wooden blocks,
And towers that touch imaginary skies.
A fearless rider on his father's knee,
An eager listener unto stories told
At the Round Table of
the nursery,
Of heroes and adven-
tures manifold.
There will be other towers
for thee to build;
There will be other
steeds for thee to ride;
There will be other leg-
ends, and all filled
With greater marvels
and more glorified.
Build on, and make thy
castles high and fair,

Rising and reaching upward to the skies;
Listen to voices in the upper air,
Nor lose thy simple faith in mysteries.
-Henry Wadsworth Longfellow

Fairytales do come true

Children

Bitter are the tears of a child: Sweeten them. Deep are the thoughts of a child: Quiet them. Sharp is the grief of a child: Take it from him. Soft is the heart of a child: Do not harden it.

-Pamela Glenconner

Children's Eye's

What kind of world is it, my friend,
that little children see?
I wonder if they see God first
because they just believe?
Do they see strength in caring eyes
who watch them as they play
Or maybe love through gentle hands
that guide them on their way?
Do children dream of future times
when they would be a king
Or just enjoy their present life
while with their friends they sing?
And when the day is over
as they close their eyes to sleep

Do they look forward
to tomorrow
with its promises
to keep?
If this is what
our children see
then it should be
no surprise -
the world would
be a better place
if we all had
children's eyes
-Tom Krause ©

106

CHILDREN QUOTES

A father is someone who carries pictures where his money used to be. -Lion

A happy childhood can't be cured. Mine'll hang around my neck like a rainbow. -Calisher

A torn jacket is soon mended; but hard words bruise the heart of a child. -Longfellow

All kids need is a little help, a little hope and somebody who believes in them. -"Magic" Johnson

And do respect the women of the world; remember you all had mothers. -Allen Toussaint

Babies do not want to hear about babies. They like to be told of giants and castles, and of somewhat which can stretch and stimulate their little minds. -Samuel Johnson

Before I got married, I had six theories about bringing up children. Now, I have six children and no theories. -John Wilmot, Earl of Rochester

By the time the youngest children have learned to keep the house tidy, the oldest grandchildren are on hand to tear it to pieces. -C. Morley

Child rearing myth #1: Labor ends when the baby is born.

All children wear the sign: "I want to be important NOW." Many of our juvenile delinquency problems arise because nobody reads the sign. -D. Pursuit

Children are our most valuable natural resource —Herbert Hoover

Children are remarkable for their intelligence and ardor, for their curiosity, their intolerance of shams, the clarity and ruthlessness of their vision. -Aldous Huxley

Children are the sum of what mothers contribute to their lives.

Diaper backward spells repaid. Think about it. -Marshall McLuhan

Don't demand respect as a parent. Demand civility and insist on honesty. But respect is something you must earn -with kids as well as with adults. -William Attwood

God couldn't be everywhere, so he created mothers. -Jewish proverb

To be in your children's memories tomorrow, you have to be in their lives today.

My life has meaning. my life has love. my life has you. my child.

Grown-ups never understand anything for themselves, and it is tiresome for children to be always and forever explaining things to them. -Antoine de Saint-Exupery

Human beings are the only creatures that allow their children to come back home. -Bill Cosby

I have found the best way to give advice to your children is to find out what they want and then advise them to do it. -Harry S Truman

If evolution really works, how come mothers only have two hands? -Milton Berle

If there is a measure of good parenthood, it could be when your children exceed your own achievements. -Haggai

In raising my children, I have found my soul.

If we don't stand up for children, then we don't stand for much. -Marian Edelman

If you bungle raising your children, I don't think whatever else you do well matters very much. -Jacqueline Kennedy Onassis

If you want a baby, have a new one. Don't baby the old one. -Jessamyn West

Infancy conforms to nobody: all conform to it, so that one babe commonly makes four or five out of the adults who prattle and play to it. -Ralph Waldo Emerson

Life affords no greater responsibility, no greater privilege, than the raising of the next generation. -C. Everett Koop

Never help a child with a task at which he feels he can succeed. -Maria Montessori

• • • • • • • • • • • • • • • • • •

🖐 Childhood is over the moment a puddle is viewed as an obstacle rather than an opportunity -Helen M Nocivelli

🖐 Too often we give children answers to remember rather than problems to solve. -Roger Lewin

🖐 When dealing with a child, keep all your wits about you and sit on the floor. -Austin O'Malley

🖐 When I approach a child, he inspires in me two sentiments; tenderness for what he is, and respect for what he may become. -Louis Pasteur

🖐 Who takes the child by the hand takes the mother by the heart. -German Proverb

🖐 Your children are not your children. They are the sons and daughters of Life's longing for itself. -Kahlil Gibran

🖐 Wouldn't it be wonderful to be as brilliant as our children thought we were when they were young, and only half as stupid as they think we are when they're teenagers? -Daisy Brown

🖐 You can learn many things from children. How much patience you have, for instance. -F. Jones

🖐 You have to love your children unselfishly. That's hard, but it's the only way. -Barbara Bush

🖐 You know children are growing up when they start asking questions that have answers.

🖐 What war is to man, childbirth is to woman. -Hindu proverb

Children's Titles

- #1 Kid of the Year
- 2 hot 2 handle
- A Berry Sweet Day
- A Candid Moment
- A Day in the life of (name)
- A Day Spent with Mickey & Minnie
- A Doll's House
- A face only a mother can love (kids making faces)
- A Hug a Day keeps the Meanies Away
- A Little Dirt Never Hurt
- A Stumble Is Not a Fall
- A chip off the old block
- ABCDEFG - tell me what you think of me!
- Accidents happen
- Adventure time
- Ain't I cute, sweet
- Ain't I Something!
- All About Me
- All By Myself
- All Clean?...I thought you said mean!
- All dressed up and ready to go
- All God's children
- All Grown Up
- All I Wanna Do Is Have Some Fun
- All my children
- All Things Bright and Beautiful
- All things grow with Love
- All Wrapped up
- Almost Famous
- Always Perfect
- Another day
- Another Sugar

• • • • • • • • • • • • • • • • • •

- ✗ Anything you can do I can do better
- ✗ Apple of my eye
- ✗ Around the House
- ✗ As time goes by
- ✗ Backyard Fun
- ✗ Barefoot in the Park
- ✗ Barefootin' Children
- ✗ Barney Made me do It
- ✗ Be All You Can Be
- ✗ Be bold - color outside the lines!
- ✗ Bear'ly Dressed
- ✗ Bear'ly One years old
- ✗ Beary Special
- ✗ Beautiful Dreamer
- ✗ Being Cute
- ✗ Bless the Beasts and Children
- ✗ Bless the Child
- ✗ Blooming beauty
- ✗ Book Worms
- ✗ Bootiful
- ✗ Born to build
- ✗ Born to Cause Trouble
- ✗ Bottomless pit
- ✗ Brief Encounters
- ✗ Brush-a Brush-a Brush
- ✗ Building Special memories
- ✗ Busy as a Beaver
- ✗ But Mom!
- ✗ Button, button, who's got the button?
- ✗ Catching a Few Zzzzzz
- ✗ Caught in the act
- ✗ Caution Kids Crossing
- ✗ Caution, Mom is Stressed
- ✗ Childhood is a journey, not a race
- ✗ Children are like leaves...They Come in Many Colors
- ✗ Children are love

112

- Children are Poor Men's Riches
- Children are the Flowers in the Garden of Life
- Children learn what they live
- Children put a twinkle in your eyes and a smile in your heart
- Choo-Choo
- Chow Time
- Circles Of Love
- Clean as a Whistle
- Close your Little Sleepy Eyes...
- Color the World With Crayons
- Color the world with love
- Comic Adventures
- Computer Whiz!
- Cool Kids
- Couch Potato
- Cowboys don't take baths... We just dust off.
- Cow'nt your blessings
- Crash and burn
- Cruisin' Along
- Cuddle Bugs
- Cute as a Bug
- Cute as a button
- Cute as can be
- Cute but Dangerous
- Cute things I say & Do
- Cute, cute, cute!
- Cutest Little Pumpkin in the Patch
- Daddy's Helper
- Daddy's Little Buddy
- Dad's #1 Fan
- Days of our lives
- Did You Ever Have to Make Up Your Mind?
- Discover Life... Have Wild Kids
- Doggone cute
- Don't Cry over Spilled Milk

* Down to Earth
* Easier said than done
* Everybody Have Fun Tonight
* Forget the dog, beware of our kids
* From the Moment I saw you I knew it would be a Grand Adventure!
* Fun and games
* Fun days
* Fun in the Mud
* Fun in the Sun
* Fun with friends
* Fun, Fun, Fun
* Funny Face, I Love You!
* Funny Faces of...
* Fun-sational
* Games Baby Plays
* Gettin' Goofy
* Going Wild
* Got Dirt?

* Grass Stains
* Growing up is hard to do
* Hangin' Out
* Happy Times
* Have Some Fun
* Havin' a Ball, Y'all
* Heart Tugs!
* Helping Hand
* Here's looking at you kid
* Here's The Scoop
* Hop Hop, we like to hop, We like to hop on Pop!
* Horsin' Around
* Hot Shots
* How Fun Thou Art
* How Time Flies
* I Am a Child of God
* I am Papa's/Nana's Kid
* I am an only kid
* I am the big brother
* I am the big sister

- I am the little brother
- I am the little sister
- I Believe!
- I did this all by myself
- I give wet kisses!
- I Know What I Like
- I love my Daddy
- I love my Mommy
- I Love You
- I want it and I want it now
- I Want to Hold Your Hand
- I'm sorry
- I'm trouble with a capital T
- If I can reach it, I'll touch it
- I'll do it myself
- I'm A Big Kid Now
- I'm a Heartbreaker
- I'm as lucky as can be, for the world's best dad belongs to me

- I'm helping mommy
- I'm so busy, my Mom's head is spinning
- I'm so cool!
- I'm Special
- I'm the only one like me
- Inside the Mind of a Child
- Inside, Outside, Upside Down
- It runs in the family
- It's All Small Stuff
- It's been a rough day
- It's Just my Imagination
- It's the little things in life that matter
- Jesus Loves Me
- Jesus Loves the Little Children
- Jumpin' for Joy
- Just a swingin'
- Just another day

- ✗ Just Hangin' around
- ✗ Just Me and My Dad!
- ✗ Just Try and Catch Me
- ✗ Kid at play
- ✗ Kids' Choice Award
- ✗ Kids Will Be Kids
- ✗ Kids Zone
- ✗ Let me do it myself
- ✗ Let the Fun Begin
- ✗ Let's go outside!
- ✗ Live Wire
- ✗ Look at _____ go!
- ✗ Me and My Shadow
- ✗ Me and My Toys
- ✗ Miles to go before I sleep
- ✗ Mom, I'll always love you, but I'll never forgive you for cleaning my face with spit on a hanky
- ✗ Mommy I Want... Pease?
- ✗ Monkeyin' Around
- ✗ More, More, More
- ✗ Mother's Little Helper
- ✗ Motor Mouth
- ✗ Much Ado About Nothing
- ✗ My favorite people
- ✗ My Favorite Things
- ✗ My fingers may be small, but I can still wrap daddy around them
- ✗ My Helper
- ✗ My Little Charmers
- ✗ My little ray of sunshine
- ✗ My many-colored days
- ✗ My name is NO but grandma calls me precious.
- ✗ No earthly joys could bring more pleasure
- ✗ No Whining
- ✗ On the Go
- ✗ Only in a world of love can we unfold and bloom.

- ⚘ Our Rising Star
- ⚘ Outdoor Fun
- ⚘ Over-exposed
- ⚘ Peek a boo! I see you!
- ⚘ Play is hard Work
- ⚘ Playing around the playground
- ⚘ Playing Dirty
- ⚘ Playing Dress-Up
- ⚘ Playing hard
- ⚘ Playing With My Toys
- ⚘ Playtime
- ⚘ Precious Treasures
- ⚘ Preschool Blues
- ⚘ Pretending is Fun
- ⚘ Pretty Cheeky
- ⚘ Put Me In Coach
- ⚘ Put Your Hand in the Hand
- ⚘ Reach high and touch the stars
- ⚘ Say it Loud! We're Cute—We're Proud!
- ⚘ Saturday in the Park
- ⚘ See _____, See _____ Play
- ⚘ See what I can do
- ⚘ Shake your sillies out
- ⚘ Sidewalk Chalk Art
- ⚘ Slippin' and Slidin'
- ⚘ Smart as a Whip
- ⚘ Snowflakes and little girls (or boys) - there are one of a kind
- ⚘ So many toys, so many choices
- ⚘ Something about that face
- ⚘ Strike a Pose
- ⚘ Swingin' Around
- ⚘ Take Me Out To The Ball game
- ⚘ Take time for the little things
- ⚘ That's Life
- ⚘ The adventures of..
- ⚘ The Little Riders

- The dog may invite you in, but the kids will scare you away
- The Littlest Angel
- The Marvelous Toy
- The More the Merrier
- The way you do the things you do
- The Wild Bunch
- These are a few of my favorite things
- These children were raised on home grown love
- Thou Shalt Not Whine
- Time for Fun
- Too busy for the grass to grow under our feet
- Too Cute for Words
- Too Much Fun
- Toy Story
- Toy, Toys - I want more toys
- Toyland
- Turn on the Fun
- Up, Up, and Away
- Warning! Children at Play!
- We'll Have Fun, Fun, Fun
- We're Havin' Some Fun Now
- What a Day!
- What a Doll
- What a Face!
- What fun!
- Wheee!
- When I grow up I want to be...
- Where's the action?
- Wild and Crazy Kids
- Wild Thing
- Yes sir, that's my baby
- Yes, hugs are good!
- You are one in a Million
- You are so beautiful!
- You Ought to Be In Pictures

In the twilight of your childhood
may the memories linger long
to be carefree and innocent
is what will keep you young
don't worry over silly stuff
that doesn't mean that much
just focus on the blessings
that are right within your touch
because my darling daughters
time will fly so swiftly past
you'll wonder where it all went
and how you grew up so fast
your grandma used to tell me
when i was young like you
that all the dreams I hope for
sometimes do come true
remember this my sweethearts
that mother loves you too
i pray for your success in life
knowing God will see you through
my fervent prayer for you this year
is that you will seek His face
for no matter where life leads you
may it be by his guiding grace
you have always been the best in me
i've been blessed beyond compare
God gave to me the gift of you
and a love that is so rare
so on this Christmas morning
will you take this gift of love
a treasure i bestow on you
sent to me from our father above
-Linda LaTourelle ©

I'll keep you right here in my heart and I'll memorize each little part

119

Monday's child is fair of face;
Tuesday's child is full of grace;
Wednesday's child is on the go;
Thursday's child is a joy to know.
Friday's child is loving and giving;
Saturday's child takes joy in living;
but the child that is born
on the Sabbath day
is merry and blithe
and bright and gay.

Growing

Growing
in
Love

☺ All Grown Up

☺ All things grow with love

☺ Getting Bigger Inch by Inch

☺ Grow n' grow n' grow

☺ Grown' like a weed

☺ Growing by leaps and bounds

☺ Growing like a weed

☺ Growing Pains

☺ I'm a big kid now

☺ Keeps growing and growing

☺ Look Who's Growing Up

☺ Ready or not, here I grow!

☺ Room to Grow

☺ Watch and See How I Grow...

The Whispers Of A Child

A child's love is like a
whisper,
given in little ways we
do not hear.
But if you listen
closely
it will be very clear.
They often do not say
it loud, but in how
they come to you...
Daddy, will you play
with me?
Mommy, tie my shoe?
The many ways they tell you,
changes as they grow.
Dad, I made the team today!
Mom, I've got to go!
Pop, I need some money,
You see there's...this
girl at school.
Mama, I met a boy today
and Wow, he's so cool!
Dad, I've got some-
thing to tell you...
I think she is the one!
Mom, he asked me to
marry him.
Would you love him as
your son?
Dad, I've got some

news for you...
It's going to be a boy!
Mom, I'm kind of
scared of this,
yet I'm filled with joy!
A child's love is like a
whisper,
given in little ways we
do not hear.
But if you listen closely,
it will be very clear.
They often do not say
it loud, but in how
they come to you...
Grandpa, will you play
with me?
Grandma, tie my shoe?
It is never ending;
a blessing from above.
Listen to the whispers
of a child's love
-S. E Chan

THE CIRCUS DAY PARADE

Oh, the Circus Day parade! How the Bugles played and played!
And how the glossy horses tossed their flossy manes, and neighed,
As the rattle and rhyme of the tenor-drummer's time
Filled all the hungry hearts of us with melody sublime

-James Whitcomb Riley

- ✿ Clowning Around At The Circus
- ✿ Clowning Around
- ✿ Under The Big Top
- ✿ Just a clown at heart
- ✿ Pop Goes the Weasel
- ✿ Lions and tigers and bears, oh my!
- ✿ March to the Music
- ✿ Strike up the band

Classic Poems

Little boy blue
The little toy dog is covered with dust,
But sturdy and staunch he stands;
And the little toy soldier is red with rust,
And his musket moulds in his hands.
Time was when the little toy dog was new,
And the soldier was passing fair;
And that was the time when our Little Boy Blue
Kissed them and put them there.

"Now, don't you go till I come," he said,
"And don't you make any noise!"
So, toddling off to his trundle-bed,
He dreamt of the pretty toys;
And, as he was dreaming, an angel song
Awakened our Little Boy Blue—
Oh! The years are many, the years are long,
But the little toy friends are true!

Aye, faithful to Little Boy Blue they stand,
Each in the same old place—
Awaiting the touch of a little hand,
The smile of a little face;
And they wonder,
as waiting the long years through
In the dust of that little chair,
What has become of our Little Boy Blue,
Since he kissed them and put them there.
-Eugene Fields

The Land of Thus and So

How would Willie like to go
To the Land of Thus-and So?
Everything is proper there
All the children comb their hair
Smoother than the fur of cats,
Or the nap of high silk hats;
Every face is clean and white
As a lily washed in light;
Never vaguest soil or speck
Found on forehead, throat or neck
Every little crimpled ear,
In and out, as pure and clear
As the cherry-blossom's blow
In the Land of Thus-and-so.
"Little boys that never fall
Down the stairs, or cry at all
Doing nothing to repent,
Watchful and obedient;
Never hungry, nor in hast
Tidy shoestrings always laced;
Never button rudely torn.
From its fellows all unworn;
Knickerbockers always new
Ribbon, tie, and collar, too;
Little watches, worn like men,
Always promptly half past 10
Just precisely right, you know,

For the Land of Thus-and So!

"And the little babies there
Give no one the slightest care
Nurse has not a thing to do
But be happy and sigh 'Boo!'
While manna just nods, and knows
Nothing but to doze and doze:
Never litter round the grate;
Never lunch or dinner late;
Never any household din
Peals without or rings within
Baby coos nor laughing calls
On the stairs or through the halls
Just Great Hushes to and fro
Pace the Land of Thus-and-So!
"Oh! the Land of Thus-and-So!–
Isn't it delightful, though?"
"Yes," lisped Willie, answering me
Somewhat slow and doubtfully
"Must be awful nice, but I
Rather wait till by and by
'Fore I go there—maybe when
I be dead I'll go there then.—
But "—The troubled little efface
Closer pressed in my embrace
"Let's don't never ever go
To the Land of Thus-and-So!"
-Eugene Field

The Land of Nod

From breakfast on through all the day
At home among my friends I stay,
But every night I go abroad
Afar into the land of Nod.

All by myself I have to go,
With none to tell me what to do--
All alone beside the streams
And up the mountain-sides of dreams.

The strangest things are these for me,
Both things to eat and things to see,
And many frightening sights abroad
Till morning in the land of Nod.

Try as I like to find the way,
I never can get back by day,
Nor can remember plain and clear
The curious music that I hear.
-Robert Louis Stevenson

Whole Duty of Children

A child should always say what's true
And speak when he is spoken to,
And behave mannerly at table;
At least as far as he is able.
-Robert Louis Stevenson

THE SUGARPLUM TREE

Have you ever heard of the Sugarplum tree?
'T is a marvel of great renown!
It blooms on the shore of the Lollipop Sea
In the garden of Shuteye Town;
The fruit that it bears is so wondrously sweet
(As those who have tasted it say)
That good little children have only to eat
Of that fruit to be happy next day.

When you've go to the tree, you would have a hard time
To capture the fruit which I sing;
The tree is so tall that no person could climb
To the boughs where the sugarplums swing!
But up in that tree sits a chocolate cat,
And a gingerbread dog prowls below—
And this is the way you contrive to get at
Those sugarplums tempting you so:
You say but the word to that gingerbread dog
And he barks with such terrible zest

That the chocolate cat is at once all agog,
As her swelling proportions attest.
And the chocolate cat goes cavorting around
From this leafy limb unto that,
And the sugarplums tumble, of course, to the ground—
Hurray for that chocolate cat!

There are marshmallows, gumdrops, and peppermint canes
With stipings of scarlet or gold,
And you carry away of the treasure that rains
As much as your apron can hold!
So come, little child, cuddle closer to me
In your dainty white nightcap and gown,
And I'll rock you away to that Sugarplum Tree
In the garden of Shuteye Town.

-Eugene Field

At the Sea-side

When I was down beside the sea
A wooden spade they gave to me
To dig the sandy shore.

My holes were empty like a cup.
In every hole the sea came up,
Till it could come no more.

-Robert Louis Stevenson

Bed in Summer

In winter I get up at night
And dress by yellow candle-light.
In summer quite the other way,
I have to go to bed by day.

I have to go to bed and see
The birds still hopping on the tree,
Or hear the grown-up people's feet
Still going past me in the street.

And does it not seem hard to you,
When all the sky is clear and blue,
And I should like so much to play,
To have to go to bed by day?

-Robert Louis Stevenson

Happy Thought

The world is so full of a number of things,
I'm sure we should all
be as happy as kings.

-Robert Louis Stevenson

OVER THE HILLS AND FARAWAY

Over the hills and far away,
A little boy steals from his morning play,
And under the blossoming apple-tree
He lies and he dreams of the things to be:
Of battles fought and of victories won,
Of wrongs o'erthrown and of great deeds done—
Of the valor that he shall prove some day,
Over, the hills and far away—
Over the hills and far away!

Over the hills and far away
It's, oh, for the toil the livelong day!
But it mattereth not to the soul aflame
With a love for riches and power and fame!
On, O man! While the sun is high—
On to the certain joys that lie
Yonder where blazeth the noon of day,
Over the hills and far away—
Over the hills and far away!

Over the hills and far away,
And old man lingers at close of day;
Now that his journey is almost done,
His battles fought and his victories won—
The old-time honesty and truth,
The trustfulness and the friends of youth,
Home and mother—where are they?
Over the hills and far away—
Over the years and far away!

-Eugene Field

THE DUEL

The gingham dog and the calico cat
Side by side on the table sat;
'Twas half-past twelve, and (what do you think!)
Nor one nor t'other had slept a wink!
The old Dutch clock and the Chinese plate
Appeared to know as sure as fate
There was going to be a terrible spat
(I wasn't there; I simply state
What was told to me by the Chinese plate!)
The Gingham dog went "bow-wow-wow!"
And the calico cat replied "mee-ow!"
The air was littered, an hour or so,
With bits of gingham and calico,
While the old Dutch clock in the chimney-place
Up with its hands before its face,
For it always dreaded a family row!
(Now mind: I'm only telling you
What the old Dutch clock declares is true!)
The Chinese plate looked very blur,
And wailed, "Oh, dear! What shall we do!"
But the gingham dog and the calico cat
Wallowed this way and tumbled that,
Employing every tooth and claw
In the awfullest way you ever saw—
And, oh! How the gingham and calico flew!
Don't fancy I exaggerate—
I got my news from the "Chinese plate!)
Next morning, where the two had sat
They found no trace of dog or cat;
And some folks think unto this day
That burglars stole that pair away!
But the truth about the cat and pup
Is this: they ate each other up!
Now what do you really think of that!
The old Dutch clock it told me so,
And that is how I came to know.
                                   -Eugene Field

Colors

Red Yellow Blue
Orange green Purple

- ☆ All the colors of the rainbow
- ☆ Can you paint with all the colors of the wind?
- ☆ A coat of many colors
- ☆ Color My World With Love
- ☆ Showing your true colors
- ☆ Blue Moon
- ☆ Blue Skies
- ☆ The grass is always greener
- ☆ The wearing of the green

- ☆ Pretty and Pink
- ☆ Perfectly Pink
- ☆ Deep Purple
- ☆ Mellow Yellow
- ☆ Yellow Brick Road
- ☆ Scarlett ribbons
- ☆ Ruby Red Shoes
- ☆ Orange Blossom
- ☆ Orange Sunset
- ☆ White as Snow

Red is the color of my true love's heart
Blue is the ocean so grand
Purple are the mountains so majestic
Orange is the color of joy
Yellow is the sun when it smiles
White is the color of gentle
Brown is chocolate and oh, so yummy
Pink sugar kisses from sweet little lips
Gold is the touch of the masters hand.
Together they make a beautiful land!
-Linda LaTourelle

Cowboys

Dear Lord up above,
Please listen on my behalf
Help my mom understand,
That cowboys don't take baths!!

- Yee ha!
- Giddy Up
- Ropin' the wind
- Ride 'em Cowboy
- Sceedaddle ya lil doggies
- Long Hard Day in the Saddle
- Head 'em up and move 'em out
- There is a new Cowboy in Town!
- Mama's don't let your baby's grow up to be cowboys

Crawling

The time before you knew my voice
Seemed such a long, long while.
I couldn't wait for you to roll,
And then to sit and clap.

And now you're off and
crawling,
Not helpless in my lap!

The beginnings of all
things are small
Look at me now I'm
starting to crawl

Crying

Come, stop your crying
It will be alright
Just take my hand
Hold it tight
I will protect you
From all around you
I will be here,
Don't you cry
For one so small,
You seem so strong
My arms will hold you,
Keep you safe and warm.

AH!
Why will my dear little
girl be so cross,
And cry, and look
sulky, and pout?
To lose her sweet
smile is a terrible loss,
I can't even kiss her
without.

Little Girls Crying
All the bells were ringing
And all the birds were singing,
When Molly sat down crying
For her broken doll;
Oh, you silly Moll!
Sobbing and sighing
For a broken doll,
When all the bells are ringing
And all the birds are singing

Tears on my pillow
Love in my heart

WHAT is it that makes little Baby cry?
Come then, let mamma wipe the tear
from her eye: There—lay down your head on my
bosom—that's right, And now tell mamma what's the
matter to-night.

Laughter and Tears

- ☺ After All These Tears
- ☺ All Teary Eyed
- ☺ As Tears Go By
- ☺ Behind These Tears
- ☺ Big Boys Do Cry
- ☺ Blood, Sweat, & Tears
- ☺ Crocodile Tears
- ☺ Cry Baby
- ☺ Cry It Out
- ☺ Cry Me a River
- ☺ Cry on Cue
- ☺ Cry on My Shoulder
- ☺ A Cryin' Shame
- ☺ Hang in There
- ☺ Here Come those tears
- ☺ Mama don't allow no pouting here
- ☺ My Achy Breaky Heart
- ☺ No Whining
- ☺ Tear After Tear
- ☺ Tear Drop
- ☺ Tears of Joy
- ☺ Tears on my Pillow
- ☺ You better not pout

Dancing

Dancing and Prancing to town we go,
On the top of the wall of the town we go.
Shall we talk to the stars, or talk to the moon,
Or run along home to our dinner so soon?

THE BABY'S DANCE

Dance, little baby, dance up high:
Never mind, baby, mother is by;
Crow and caper, caper and crow,
There, little baby, there you go;
Up to the ceiling, down to the ground,
Backwards and forwards, round and round;
Then dance, little baby, and mother shall sing,
While the gay merry coral goes ding-a-ding, ding.

- All that jazz.
- Ballet Beauty
- Beautiful Ballerina
- Bop till you drop
- Dance to the music
- Dance, dance, dance
- Dancing toes
- Do a little dance
- Do you wanna dance
- Fancy Footwork
- Feet Don't fail me now
- Happy feet
- I love to dance
- I've got rhythm
- Jitterbug girl
- Keep on dancin'
- Practice makes perfect
- Recital
- Shall we dance
- Tap
- Tiny Dancer
- Toe shoes and Tutus
- Tutu cute
- Twinkle Toes

Dolls

THE LITTLE DRESSMAKER

This little girl, I'm glad to say,
Is fond of work as well as play.
From bits of ribbon, velvet, lace,
She makes nice gowns to suit each face.
Puts feathers in a bonnet tall,
And trims a hat for little Doll.
One dolly's large, the other small;
One stands alone, and one must fall.
Though dresses so nice, they won't obey;
But sit quite sullen all the day.

The little girl expects no declaration of tenderness
from her doll. She loves it, and that's all. It is thus
that we should love. –De Gourmont

You see Mr. Carpenter
My doll has grown so tall,
I really don't know what to do,
Her crib is much too small.
So I have brought it, please, to you,
To take the foot-board out.
And you must make it wider, too,
For dolly's growing stout.

Baby's Dolly

Shining eyes, very blue,
Opened very wide;
Yellow curls, very stiff,
Hanging side by side;
Chubby cheeks, very pink;
Lips red as holly;
No ears, and only thumbs-
That's baby's dolly.

Dolls

In the dell of our garden,
My dolls and I take tea
And days when I have raisins
The catbirds dine with me

Hush, baby, my dolly,
I pray you don't cry.
I'll give you some bread
And some milk by and by
Or perhaps you like custard
Or maybe a tart.
Than to either you're welcome,
With all of my heart.

Dolly and me
Sat sipping tea
And eating cake
That momma made
The sun was bright
And life a delight!

 I can hardly wait 'til nighttime falls, when I crawl into bed with my favorite dolls.

 I have a doll from days gone by -very worn and tattered. But she was there for me to love and that's all that really mattered.

 I'm just a Raggedy Ann in a Barbie Doll world.

 You're never too old to play with dolls.

Up in the early morning,
Just at the peep of day,
Driving the sleep from my eyelids,
Pulling the quilts away;
Pinching my cheeks and my forehead
With his soft fingers small;
This is my bright-eyed darling,
This is my baby doll.

Down on the floor in the parlor,
Creeping with laugh and shout,
Or out in the kitchen and pantry,
Tossing the things about;
Rattling the pans and the kettles,
Scratching the table and wall;
This is my roguish darling,
This is my baby doll

Nestling up close to my bosom,
Laying his cheek to mine,
Covering my mouth with his kisses
Sweeter than golden wine,
Flinging his white arms about me,
Soft as the snow-flakes fall;
This is my cherished darling,
This is my baby doll.

Dearer, a thousand times dearer,
The wealth in my darling I hold,
Than all the earth's glittering treasure,
Its glory, and honours, and gold;
If these at my feet were now lying,
I'd gladly renounce them all,
For the sake of my bright-eyed darling,
My dear little baby doll.
-B. Thompson

138

Dress Up

🎎 Looking This Beautiful is Hard Work

🎎 Lovely Lips

🎎 Make over

🎎 Marvelous Makeover

🎎 Rosy Cheeks

🎎 Something About that Face

🎎 What a Face

The Tea Party

In the pleasant
green Garden
We sat down to tea:
"Do you take
sugar?" and
"Do you take
milk?"
She'd got a new gown on—
A smart one of silk.
We all were as happy
As happy could be,
On that bright Summer's day
When she asked us to tea.

• • • • • • • • • • • • • • • • •

EARTH

There is a garden in every childhood,
An enchanted place
Where colors are brighter, the air softer,
And the morning
More fragrant than ever again.
-Elizabeth Lawrence

If you want children
to keep their feet on the ground,
Put some responsibility on their shoulders.
-Abigail Van Buren

There are two lasting bequests
we can give our children;
One is roots. The other wings.
-Holding Carter, Jr.

 Every child is born a naturalist.
His eyes are, by nature,
Open to the glories of the stars,
The beauty of the flowers,
And the mystery of life.
-R. Search

Usually children spend more time in the
Garden than anybody else.
It is where they learn about the world,
Because they can be in it
Unsupervised, yet protected.

I'm Glad the Sky is Painted Blue

I'm glad the sky is painted blue,
And the earth is painted green,
With such a lot of nice fresh air
All sandwiched in between.
-Anonymous

The Rainbow

Can that fairy place be found
Where the rainbow touches ground?
Will you tell me, driver, pray,
Is it many miles away?

Somewhere there must be a spot
Shining like a colored blot,
Pink and purple, blue and green,
Like a transformation scene.

What must all the cattle think
When the grass and flowers turn pink?
Woolly sheep, what do you do
When the daisies field shines blue?

Happy must those children be,
Who the rainbow's end can see,
Who can play and dance and sing
In the rainbow's shining ring!

Little drops of water,
Little grains of sand
Make the mighty ocean
And the beauteous land
And the little moments,
Humble though they be,
Make the mighty ages
Of eternity.

The Cuckoo

Cuckoo flowers and daisies,
Grasses grey with dew,
Sunbeams of buttercups,
And a sky all blue.

Primroses and cowslips,
Bluebells and sweet may,
And a cuckoo calling
Far, far away.

Forget-me-nots and cresses,
In the streamlet blue,
Fly a little nearer,
O Cuckoo, do!

Eating

Messy Matilda & Starvin Marvin
Yum-Yum, fillin' my tum

Slurp, Slurp

Spaghetti, Spaghetti all over the place.
Up to my elbows. Up to my face.
But it tastes so warm and yummy
Filling my mouth and my tummy.

Lunchtime Delights

There's a girl in my class
Ethel McSporidge
Who brings sandwiches filled with
Jam and cold porridge
She says that they're nice
And would I like a chew
But I always say, "No"
I think you would too
'Cause I think jam and porridge
Doesn't sound very nice
It's a bit like stale pizza
With three week old rice
So I think I will stay
With my own if you please
A delicate mixture of
Fish and hen's knees

-Rob Erskine © (See Bio)

Encourage

I love you so much, my beautiful child. I wish that you could see yourself, as others see you: a sensitive, intelligent person, who has all the qualities necessary to become a very successful beautiful person. One day you will look in the mirror, and see the extraordinary person that you really are, and you will understand why we think you are awesome. You are our treasure. Please remember how much you are loved and appreciated.

We love you so much, dear beautiful child,
Forever, Mother and Father

If ever things are not going well for you and every
you have some problem to solve.
If every you are feeling confused
and don't know the right thing to do.
If ever you are feeling frightened and hurt,
or if you just need someone to talk to.
Please remember that I am here for you
at all times without judgment
and with understanding and love.

Don't cry little darling
Momma's here for you
Everything that makes you sad
God will see us through

Baby Love
My prayers are with you always
Day and night

Fairies

Come up here, O dusty feet! Here is fairy bread to eat. Here in my retiring room, Children, you may dine On the golden smell of broom and pine; And when you have eaten well, Fairy stories hear and tell.
-Robert Louis Stevenson

Tiny Rock

The magical land of fairies, a magical place to see
Fairies that fly in the window and dance and twirl for me
Gowns swirl softly at their feet as they dance to a magical sound
You can feel a gentle breeze, as they twirl their wands around

Their faces glow with star dust, their fairy gowns glitter and shine
And if you ever see them, you'll wish for one more time
Tiny feet clad in slippers, with bells hanging from the toes
You'll hear a tinkling jingle, each time they touch their nose

They scamper like mice through the tall grass,
They skip and they bounce and they hop
They stop long enough to wink shyly,
As they as give a cute little laugh

Tiny feet dance through the forest,
At night you can hear the sweet sound
Of fairies tucked snug in the garden,
In flower beds they can be found
-Sandra Prouse © (See Bio)

When the first baby laughed, the laugh broke into thousands of pieces and they all skipped about. That was the beginning of fairies.

• • • • • • • • • • • • • • • • • • • •

Willow

Fairies in their flower skirts by a misty pond
Planting a multitude of flower seeds
to grow all summer long
Sprinkling them with fairy dust to make a garden grow
A paradise of flowers In the forest where they sow

Hummingbirds and bumble bees set a pattern of delight
Fluttering through the forest on golden wings of flight
Lavender and yellow, blue and pastel pink
Skirts made of shamrocks, the color emerald silk

Floating neath a willow, with branches reaching down
To lift the fairies gently, right up off the ground
Sunflowers and dewdrops, bachelor buttons too
Scattered through the forest in a rainbow colored hue

Morning glories lift their heads and open sleepy eyes
Climbing up the tree trunks to catch a view of paradise
Listen to the birds sing, a tune of sweet delight
Perching on the petals, in the warm sunlight
-Sandra Prouse © (See Bio)

Freckles are fairies kisses

Family Is Love

What does the bee do?
Bring home honey.
And what does the Father do?
And what does the Mother do?
Lay out the money.
And what does baby do?
Eat up the honey.

Family Ties

Family ties are precious threads, no matter where we roam, They draw us close to those we love, and pull our hearts toward home.

A Mother's Joys

My sons are like their father dear,
And all the neighbors tell
That my young blue-eyed daughter's just
The picture o' myself.
Oh, blessings on my darling all
They're dear as summer's shine;
My heart runs o'er with happiness
To think that they are mine!

At evening, morning, every hour,
I've an unchanging prayer,
That heaven would my babies bless
My hope, my joy, my care.
I've gear enough, I've gear enough,
I've bonnie babies three
Their welfare is a mine of wealth,
Their love a crown to me.
-William Ferguson

147

Fighting

Mad at You

I'm mad at you!
You don't play fair!
You scratched my arm,
And pulled my hair!!

I'm mad at you
You don't play right!
You should be nice
And not start a fight!
And I'm sad at you
'Cause I like to play
With my big brother
Every single day!

But today I'm not going
To play with you anymore
'Cause you cheat
When you keep score!
I'm mad at you
And intend to stay
Mad at you
For the rest of the day.

-Thena Smith © (See Bio)

 # Flowers

From Market

OH who'll give us Posies,
And Garlands of Roses,
To twine round our heads so gay?
For here we come bringing
You many good wishes to-day,
From market - from market
We all come up from market.

Where innocent bright-eyed daisies are,
With blades of grass between,
Each daisy stands up like a star
Our of a sky of green.

My little Rosebud

To see a world in a grain of sand and a heaven in a wildflower, hold infinity in the palm of your hand and eternity in an hour. -William Blake

Flowers

A rose can say
"I Love You",
Orchids can
enthrall,
But a weed
bouquet
in a chubby fist
Oh my, that
says it all

Children in this great big world
Are flowers in a way
Some are light, some are dark
Like a real bouquet

♡

One Little Flower, One Little Bee

One little flower, one little bee.
One little blue bird, high in the tree.
One little brown bear smiling at me.
One is the number
I like, you see.

Foster Family

I do not wish to take your mother's place,
And yet my pride and pleasure are no less.
You may not be the daughter of my flesh,
But you are still the daughter of my heart.
I know my very presence in your life
Can't help but to remind you of the pain
And anger of your parents' separation.
And yet my only purpose here is love.
Stepmothers and stepdaughters are a pair
Created both by joy and by disaster.
We did not choose each other, but were chosen
By love and by the anguish of love's end.
But we can choose to love each other well,
Accepting fortune's gift with unfeigned grace.
Know as you step forth this graduation:
You have my love as long as life permits.
That it might in the will of sunlight sing.
So may we long remain through love and art:
Stepparent and stepchildren of the heart.

Child of my heart!

We are a family now, a whole,
Of which you are a part,
And you are just as much my child
As any in my heart.

I do not love you differently,
Nor would I give up less
Of all that life has given me
To bring you happiness.

Foster Children

Foster children move from place to place
With memories that walk the night alone,
Nor is the love theirs that they must embrace.
Yet most survive with a peculiar grace,
Even though their hearts should turn to stone
As they move about from place to place.
Perhaps within themselves they find a space
To furnish as they would a mobile home,
Finding scraps of things they can embrace,
A memory like some much-fingered lace,
Thoughts and dreams that only they have known,
Moving as they do from place to place,
Their childhood impossible to trace
In the years of yearning after they are grown,
Filled with love they've chosen to embrace,
Yet with their losses etched upon their face,
Pain for which no penance can atone.
How can they move and move from place to place,
Surrendering the love they must embrace?

Families come in all shapes and sizes
We are so glad that you are here
You are a perfect part of God's plan
We hold you in our heart so dear

I love you just the way you are
To me you are a shining star
We pray that you will come to know
Our heart is yours, we love you so.

SWEET SUGAR DIMPLES

Did you ever see my baby— my one, my only girl?
She is not a blue-eyed lady,
No lily, nor pearl;
But a merry little gypsy
With eyes as brown as berries,
A tiny dimple in her cheek,
And lips like luscious cherries.

-Louis Custice

Tiny new babies are everything nice.
Like peaches and cream strawberry ice.

The fruit of the Spirit is love, joy, peace, patience, kindness, goodness, faithfulness, gentleness and self-control.

-Gal. 5:15

🍎 Apple of my eye 🍎 Berry Beautiful

153

Blackberry Patch

We walked along the well worn path,
Long baked beneath the sun,
Like piece of clay in sculptor's hand,
Till satisfied it's done.
Small dusty clouds kicked by bare feet,
With each step that is taken,
Our destination known by heart,
Our purpose not mistaken.
Around a bend, then straight ahead,
Blackberry patch in view,
With berries plump and sweet to tongue,
Still wet with morning dew.
One for the pail, one for our mouth,
So picking was quite slow,
Not stopping till our buckets filled,
To almost overflow.
The sun now higher in the sky,
Warmed ground beneath our feet,
So that we hurried down the path,
Almost as in retreat.
No taste on earth to compare to,
A homemade berry pie,
Made with berries, all hand picked,
Made ripe by summer sky.
Years later I returned again,
To seek the place I'd known,
Faint path was all that still remained,
Where berry patch had grown.
For change had come with berries gone,
A row of houses there,
Nothing left but memories,
Of what was picked with care.
Loree (Mason) O'neil © (See Bio)

Fruit

Super
Delicious
Simply
nutritious
Are
your
sweet
kisses
To
me

154

There is a garden in every childhood, an enchanted place where colors are brighter, the air softer, and the morning more fragrant than ever again.
-Elizabeth Lawrence

To see a world in a grain of sand and a heaven in a wild-flower, hold infinity in the palm of your hand and eternity in an hour.
-William Blake

Garden

In search of my mothers garden, I found my own.
-Alice Walker

Come Play in the Garden

Little sister, come away,
And let us in the garden play,
For it is a pleasant day.
On the grass-plat let us sit,
Or, if you please, we'll play a bit,
And run about all over it.
But the fruit we will not pick,
For that would be a naughty trick,
And very likely make us sick.
Nor will we pluck the pretty flowers
That grow about the beds and bowers,
Because you know they are not ours.
We'll take the daisies, white and red,
Because mamma has often said
That we may gather them instead.
And much I hope we always may
Our very dear mamma obey,
And mind whatever she may say.
-Jane Taylor

Garden

Look and see my darling!
Baby do you hear?
Joy is in the garden today.
'Tis sweet perfume of lilacs
scenting the morning breeze
As melodious robin redbreast
awakens me with his call
The roses wind with laziness
and such a gentle ease
Oh, what a wonderful blessing,
Just like you, the beauty of it all.
--Linda LaTourelle

This is my garden,
I'll rake it with care.
Here are the flower seeds.
I'll plant in there.
The sun will shine, the rain will fall.
My garden will blossom pretty
Grow straight and tall.
Just like the garden, my baby dear
God will bless and help you grow
Guiding you with hands so strong
Oh my precious we love you so

The farmer plants the seeds.
The farmer plants the seeds.
Hi, Ho, the dairy-oh.
The farmer plants the seeds.
The sun comes out to shine...
The rain begins to fall.
The seeds begin to grow...
The farmer digs up food...
Now we get to eat!

Girls

Two Good Girls

Two good little children, named Mary and Ann,
  Both happily live, as good girls always can;
And though they are not either sullen or mute,
  They seldom or never are heard to dispute.

A bright and sunny smiling face,
  A mix of playfulness and grace,
  A fun-loving and friendly way,
  Of bringing joy to every day,
  Her little hugs and kisses, too,
The way she works her wiles on you
And sets your heart all in a whirl
These are the charms of a little girl

A girl is Innocence playing in the mud, Beauty standing on its head, and Motherhood dragging a doll by the foot. -Allan Beck

The little girl expects no declaration of tenderness from her doll. She loves it, and that's all. It is thus that we should love. -De Gourmont

Sugar and spice and everything nice, that's what little girls are made of.

Whoever said diamonds are a girls best friend, didn't have a baby doll.

Rink a Dink Dink, A Little Girl in pink

Hey! Did you happen to see the most beautiful girl in the world!

157

G (girl)—gabby, generous, gentle, genuine, gifted, giddy, giggle, giving, gleeful, go-getter, good, goofy, goose, gorgeous, graceful, gracious, grand, great, grimy, grin, groovy, growing, growing up, grumpy

Giggles and curls, ribbons and bows
she's so adorable from her head to her toes!

A Girl is...
A joy bringer
A heart warmer
A memory maker

A Girl is...
Love.

Little girls are precious gifts,
wrapped in love serene.
Their dresses tied with sashes
and futures tied with dreams.

I had a little tea party this afternoon at three.
'Twas very small, three guests in all,
Just I, myself and me.
Myself ate up the sandwiches,
While I drank up the tea.
'Twas also I who ate the pie,
And passed the cake to me.

So
Pretty

There was a little girl who
had a little curl
Right in the middle
of her forehead,
When she was good, she
was very, very good,
But when she was bad
she was horrid.

Little Lucy

A little child, six summers old,
So thoughtful and so fair
There seemed about her pleasant ways
A more that childish air,
Was sitting on a summer's eve
Beneath a spreadin' tree,
Intent upon an ancient book
That lay upon her knee.

She turned each page with careful hand,
And strained her sight to see,
Until the drowsy shadows slept
Upon the grassy lea;
Then closed the book, and upward looked
And straight began to sing
A simple verse of hopeful love

I enjoy being a girl

There's nothing like the touch of love

BABY GIRL

Nestled sweetly in your arms,
Is a touch of the Father's love.
A tiny, slumbering baby girl,
Fresh from Heaven above.
Cherish each tender moment,
As you look on her tiny face;
For you're holding a priceless treasure,
Wrapped in ribbons, roses and lace.
Soon, this tiny bundle of pink,
Will grow into a little girl;
With baby dolls and dress up clothes,
And a ballerina twirl.
With a sparkle in her laughing eyes,
She'll steal your heart away.
So hold tight to this special gift,
And memories of this day.
-Alison Coxsey © (See Bio)

Little Girls

Little rays of sunshine
In their mother's pearls
Sweet bits of Heaven
With pony tail or curls!

A little bit like their mommy
But full of babyish charms
They love to be snuggled up by Daddy
Held tightly in his arms.
-Thena ©

- Think Pink
- Pinkadelic
- In The Pink
- Princess Of Pink
- Pink Princess
- Pink Perfection
- Pinkilicious
- Pretty In Pink
- Pink Panther
- Pink-A-Boo
- Tickled Pink
- A Beary Special Girl
- Ain't She Cute
- Ain't She Sweet
- All American Girl
- All Dolled Up
- All Girl
- American Beauty
- American Girl
- Bad Hair Day
- Big Girls Do Cry
- Big Girls Don't Cry
- Blondie
- Blooming Beauty
- Brown Eyed Girl
- Buttons & Bows
- Daddy's Girl
- Everything Nice
- Funny Girl
- Girls Will Be Girls
- Has Anybody Seen My Gal?
- Hello, Pretty Girl
- I Saw Her Standing There
- Isn't She Lovely
- It's a Girl
- Just one of the girls
- Just the Girls
- Little girls are so very special!
- Little Lady
- Mommy's Little Babydoll
- More Spice Than Sugar
- More Sugar Than Spice
- My Bonnie Lassie

♡ My Favorite Brunette

♡ My Girl

♡ My little carrot top

♡ Our Little Miss Sunshine

♡ Pretty as a Picture

♡ Prima Ballerina

♡ Ribbons and Bows

♡ Rosy Cheeks

♡ Ruffles & Lace

♡ She's a Superstar

♡ Sitting Pretty

♡ Such a wonderful girl

♡ Sugar and Spice A Whole Lotta Spice

♡ Sugar and Spice and Everything Nice

♡ Thank God I'm a Country Girl

♡ Thank Heaven For Little Girls

♡ That Girl!

♡ Uptown Girl

♡ What a Girl Needs

♡ What a Girl Wants

♡ What are Little Girls Made of?

♡ Where the Girls Are

♡ Who's That Girl?

♡ What a Beauty!

♡ You Go, Girl

♡ You Grow, Girl

♡ You must have been a beautiful baby, 'cause baby look at you now.

Thank heaven for little girls. For little girls get Bigger every day.

Grand family

Going to see Grandmamma
Little Molly and Damon
Are walking so far,
For they're going to see
Their kind Grandmamma.
And they very well know,
When they get there she'll take
From out of her cupboard
Some very nice cake.
And into her garden
They know they may run,
And pick some red currants,
And have lots of fun.

Look at your pictures and I see
A whole new world looking back at me
I wonder what life to you will bring
To watch your face with each new thing
Your mother will be there to dry your tears
To read to you and calm your fears
Your father will teach you to ride a bike
To bait a hook and to fly a kite
Set your goals high and try your wings
You have mountains to climb and bells to ring
No matter the task your asked to do
The love of your family will see you through
So as you grow with each passing day
We'll watch and hope and sometimes pray
For all of my dreams have now come true
First with my children and now through you.
-Barbara K. Cox ©

WHEN I GROW UP

When I grow up I mean to go
Where all the biggest rivers flow,
And take a ship and sail around
The seven seas until I've found
Robinson 'Crusoe's famous isle,
And there I'll land and stay a while,
And see how it would feel to be
Lord on an island in the sea

When I grow up I man tot rove
Through orange and palmetto grove,
To drive a sledge across the snow
Where great explorers go,
To hunt for treasures hid of old
Bu buccaneers and pirates bold,
And see if somewhere there may be
A mountain no one's climbed but me.

When I grow up I mean to do
The things I've always wanted to;
I don't see why grown people stay
At home when they could be away.
-Rupert Sargent Holland

When You and I Grow Up

When you and I
Grow up—Polly—
I mean that you and me,
Shall go sailing in a big ship
Right over all the sea.
We'll wait till we are older,
For if we went today,
You know that we might lose ourselves,
And never find the way.
-Kate Greenaway

Growing up is hard to do

Growing Up

I kicked and stretched and wiggled,
'Twas surprising how I grew bigger
Each day that I got bigger,
I got better looking, too!

You are the rose about to bloom,
The color soon to wake,
The perfume set to scent the breeze,
The bud about to break.
You stand upon the lip of time
Alight with what will be,
And see yourself out to the sky
Across the open sea.
We see you vertically, a gift
Too beautiful to plumb,
And treasure all the years you were
And all the years to come.

From diapers and rattles
To mud pies and puppies
Dollies and teddies
To slumber parties all night
Party dresses and perfume
To driving a car
These are the memories
I'll treasure forever

165

When I grow up I'd like to be
An explorer, brave and bold
I'd go off to the jungle
And search for hidden gold

And while I'm there
I'd wrestle with
A crocodile or two
Then capture a rhinoceros
To put in London Zoo

I'd discover a secret city
Then defy an ancient curse
Which would bring me out in blisters
On my bum or even worse!!

I'd fight off tribes of pygmies
Who'd fire arrows dipped in mud
That flew like rockets through the air
And landed with a thud

With pockets full of treasure
I'd head for home again
Dodging traps and giant snakes
Then escaping in a plane

When at last I'd reached my house
Hid the treasure in the shed
I'd have my tea, clean my teeth
And then go off to bed
-Rob Erskine © (See Bio)

I'm A Big Kid Now

Getting Bigger Everyday

Hair

Wispy curls on pretty girls
My sweet little angelic doll.
Honey pale skin and dimple chins
Surround smiles that melt the Gods.
A gift from heaven I have been blessed
As she lay upon my breast.
My life born again in those big blue eyes
So I shall never weep, for the wispy curls
On this sweet little girl are mine alone to keep.
-Shanda Purcell

Baby's Hair

Nothing more
precious to keep
In tones of
a hue so deep
As soft as a si-
lent prayer
A lock of my
baby's hair

Curly Top

Curly Locks! Curly Locks! Wilt thou be mine? Thou shalt not wash the dishes, nor yet feed the swine. But sit on a cushion and sew a fine seam and feast upon strawberries, sugar and cream.
-James Whitcomb Riley

Today is your
first haircut
And your curls so
soft and shiny
Lie in a pile upon
the floor
But I will take a
lock of gold
And place be-
tween the pages
To save forever
more

Hair

- ☺ A Cut Above
- ☺ A Whole New Look
- ☺ Bad Hair Day
- ☺ Bed Head
- ☺ Curly Top
- ☺ Do It Yourself Haircut
- ☺ Hair Art
- ☺ Heads Up
- ☺ I Have a Brand New Hair Do
- ☺ I'm still the cutest
- ☺ Letting our hair down
- ☺ New Do
- ☺ Shear Magic
- ☺ Snip Snip
- ☺ Super Cut
- ☺ The Cutting Edge
- ☺ Where's my hair
- ☺ Wiggin' Out
- ☺ Your Crowning Glory

Baby's Locks

First Haircut

I sit and watch with eagle eye
And wish I were not here
How can I bring my tiny one
To this place that causes tears?

He sits and looks at me
With such trust in his face
And handles this experience
With such precocious grace!

What an awful day it is
I really hate to say
That my darling baby boy
Gets his first haircut today!
-Thena Smith ©

Hands and Feet

No rosebuds yet by dawn impearled
Match, even in loveliest lands,
The sweetest flowers in all the world
Are those of a babies hand

- Childhood will be gone before you know it. The fingerprints on the wall appear higher and higher. Then suddenly they disappear

- A mother holds her children's hands for a short while, their hearts are hers forever.

- What feeling is so nice as a child's hand in yours?

The wonder of a miracle
From which this love began
There is so much found
In the touch of a child's hand.

Give me patience when little hands,
Tug at me with small demands,
Give me gentle words and smiling eyes
And keep my lips from sharp replies,
So in years to come when my house is still
Beautiful memories it's rooms may fill.

You wash my prints off windows and walls,
Everyday as I run, jump and play
So here is a special print to remember everyone
Made with love for you on this Mother's Day

Hands

My little hands play peekaboo
or wave and say how do you
When I fall down they pick me up
or hold my little sippy cup
My little hands reach for your hug
when I am in my bed so snug
And when my hands I fold to pray
'tis thanks I give for you today.
My little hands in time will grow
but forever will my love be so
For your big hands have held me tight
and taught me how to live just right
so take this tiny print of mine
and know that your love is divine
For I know you're there in all I do
Holding my hand and loving me true
-Linda LaTourelle © 2004

My fingers may be small,
but I can still wrap daddy around them

My Handprint

My handprint you see, is part of me,
and I want to share it with you.
So when I've grown so big and
tall you'll remember when I
was small.

LITTLE HANDS

Little hands trying to help with the dishes
Although it may go against all of our wishes
Little hands displaying their works of art
When on walls with colors they make their mark
On the floor there are pots and pans
You can bet they got there by little hands
And when you decided to dress in white
Little hands with chocolate will hold on tight
While in a store shopping they have their way
To reach out and grab a passing display
As fast as lighting as quick as a wink
They can sail a glass right into the sink
Little hands hold on with all their might
When they give you a hug as they say good night
And all the treasures from all the world's lands
Can't bring the joy found in Little Hands
-Barbara K. Cox

Treasure of Love

Ten little fingers,
Ten tiny toes,
The sweetest of smiles
And a cute little nose.
A treasure to love
And hold in your heart
Sent from above
A joy to behold!

My Sweet Pea

Tiny Hands

Morning came and I awoke,
to meet the day's demands.
Always there close by me,
Were my daughter's tiny hands.

When I would wash the dishes,
Or dry the pots and pans
On a chair beside me,
Were my daughter's tiny hands.

Cleaning was a daily chore,
In spite of my best plans.
For everywhere were images
Of my daughter's tiny hands.

Shopping was a tedious task,
Regardless of commands,
Things 'oft appeared in the cart
From my daughter's tiny hands.

When I sang my first solo,
There, sitting in the stands,
Clapping loudest of them all,
Were my daughter's tiny hands.

Sands of time have slipped away,
'Thru the hour glass they ran,
How sweet would be, once more to see,
My daughter's tiny hands.

-Brenda Ball © 2003 (See Bio)

Sometimes you get discouraged
Because I am so small
And always leave my fingerprints
On furniture and walls
But every day I'm growing
I'll be grown up some day
And all those tiny handprints
Will surely fade away
So here's a little handprint
Just so you can recall
Exactly how my fingers looked
When I was very small

☺ Pinky power

☺ Me and my thumb

☺ Thumbody Loves Me

☺ Thumbkin and Tippytoe

☺ Fingers & Toes, love grows

☺ Fingerprints on my heart

☺ Hands and hearts together

☺ Hands are for grabbing

☺ Hands, fingers, hugs & toes

☺ Helping Hands

☺ Here comes thumbkin

☺ I Want to Hold Your Hand

☺ I'm Thumbody Special!

☺ Put Your Hand in the Hand

☺ Ten Tiny Fingers and Toes

☺ Thumbwhere over the nose

☺ Hold my hand, steal my heart

Will our footprints be deep enough for our children to follow ?

• • • • • • • • • • • • • • • • • •

Thumbs and Blankies

Thumb kin good....

When I was just a baby
Before I was even born
I had a nice and cozy room
Where I was safe and warm.

My only comfort while I was there
Awaiting my arrival
Was to such my little thumb
To help in my survival.

I really found great comfort
It put me right at ease
But once I entered into the world
You wanted me to cease!

I love you so very much
And I try to do my best
But I cannot give up my thumb...
What else do you suggest???
-Thena ©

🍼 Me and my blankie   🍼 Jesus is my blankie

🍼 Security blanket   🍼 I lost my binky

🍼 Not without my woobie   🍼 My best friend, passie

🍼 Baby loves binky   🍼 Gotta love the blankie

🍼 Where's my passie?   🍼 My favorite toy

🍼 Plug it up!

🍼 I want my blankie

🍼 Give me my blankie

🍼 Don't wash my blankie

My Footprints

Today I'll run and jump
Wade in puddles having fun,
I'll walk barefoot in the grass
And play until day is done.

One day my feet may take me
To places far and wide
Wherever life will take me
I know your love is by my side

Perhaps I'll stroll upon the moon
Or run in some incredible race
Whatever I do, wherever I go
Will be by God's marvelous grace

But for now I'll leave my footprints
Soft and tender upon your heart
And one day when you miss me
May my love this gift impart.
-Linda LaTourelle ©2004

Pittypat and Tippytoe;
All day long they come and go...
Pittypat and Tippytoe;
Footprints up and down the hall,
Playthings scattered on the floor,
Finger-marks along the wall,
Tell-tale smudges on the door...
By these presents you shall know
Pittypat and Tippytoe.
Oh the thousand worrying things
Everyday recurrent brings!
Hands to scrub and hair to brush,
Search for playthings gone amiss,
Many a wee complaint to hush,
Many a little bump to kiss;
Life seems one vain, fleeting show
To Pittypat and Tippytoe!
On the floor and down the hall,
Rudely smudged upon the wall,
There are proofs in every kind
Of the havoc they have wrought,
And upon my heart you 'd find
Just such trade-marks, if you sought;
Oh, how glad I am 't is so,
Pittypat and Tippytoe!
-Eugene Field

⚘ These Foot's were made for Eatin'

⚘ The journey begins with a single step

⚘ You've got the cutest little tootsie toes

⚘ The first step begins with a fall and a bump

⚘ Too busy for the grass to grow under our feet

⚘ Walk and run, having fun, so big now

Tell me, what is half so sweet
As a baby's tiny feet,
Pink and dainty as can be,
Like a coral from the sea?
Talk of jewels strung in rows,
Gaze upon those little toes,
Fairer than a diadem,
With the mother kissing them!

Little feet, so rich with charm,
May you never come to harm.
As I bend and proudly blow
Laughter out of every toe,
This pray, that God above
Shall protect you with His love,
And shall guide those little feet
Safely down life's broader street.
-Edgar Guest

Pitter Patter of little feet

- Baby Steps
- Barefootin'
- Dancin' Feet
- First Steps
- Hot footin'
- Yep, ten toes!
- Playing Footsie
- Step by Step
- Walkin' the line
- This little Piggy

- My Little Piggies
- Sweet Little Feet
- Alive and Kicking
- Toot, toot, tootsie
- One Step at a Time
- Barefoot in the Park
- On your mark, get set, go
- Ten Tiny Fingers & Toes
- Tiptoe through my garden
- Pitter patter of little feet

A Hundred Years from Now...it will not matter what your bank account was, the sort of house you lived in, or the kind of car you drove . . . but the world may be different because you were important in the life of a child.

Hard Times

LEFTOVERS

When we were young and growing up,
We knew that we were poor,
That the hand me downs and pass me downs,
That passed through our front door,
Were just about all that we had,
And the most we could wish for,
Still they could make our eyes light up,
And cause our hearts to soar.
So many times we were hungry,
And we'd ask "What will we eat?"
And mother would smile as she told us,
"Tonight we have a treat!"
For Mrs. Jones from down the road,
Just happened to be passing by,
Bringing with her what she claimed,
Was just an extra pie.
Leftovers can fill one's tummy,
And taste like greatest feast,
While hand me downs can make one feel,
Pretty at the very least.
Growing up was not that easy,
But one lesson that we found,
there was nothing wrong with leftovers,
And there was beauty in a hand me down.
© 2003 Loree (Mason) O'Neil

Hiccups

How to get rid of hiccups:
Hold your breath till your face turns blue;
Drink a large glass of water or two;
Stand on your head with your feet in the air;
Ask someone to give you scare;
Drink something bitter;
Or drink something sweet ;
Bend way over till your hands touch your feet;
Jump up and down for an hour or so;
Sit very still and wish them to go.
Spin around and around till you can't stand up;
Try to drink hot coffee from the wrong side of the cup
Walk on the ceiling with magnetized shoes;
Listen to an hour of the evening news.
Paint your face with spots and flowers;
Listen to bagpipe music for hours.
These are my ways to make hiccups quit-
But none of them work (hic-cup)
Not one little bit (hic-cup).
-Joe Thompson © (See Bio)

Little baby Hiccup
Giggles and a giddy-up
Smiles to warm your heart
Love right from the start

HOLIDAYS

CHRISTMAS IS COMING
Christmas is coming!
Oh, my! Oh, my!
Look out, little man,
don't cry! Don't cry!
For Santa Clause loveth
a brave little boy,
And surely remembers
all such with a toy
The joy of the bells
In each bosom swells,
For the goodness of giving
makes every heart glad.

The Fate of the Gingerbread Bakers
Here are Momma and Daddy baking
Look at the little house they're making
Spiced and sugared, covered with candy
Decorating it fine and oh how dandy
Yummy little house so cute and sweet
Good enough for Santa to eat!

Make yourself a Merry Little Christmas and frost it with Love!

Christmas Titles

- ___ days 'til Christmas
- ___ shopping days left
- A Merry Little Christmas
- All I Want for Christmas
- All is Calm
- Babes in Toyland
- Baubles and Bangles
- Beary Christmas
- Beneath the Wreath
- Beware of Greeks Bearing Gifts
- Carol of the Bells
- Christ IS the BEST part of Christmas
- Christ is the Heart and Soul of Christmas
- Christmas is Heavenly
- Christmas Joy to Everyone
- Christmas Magic
- Christmas Morning
- Christmas Wishes
- Claus & Company
- Cool Yule
- Cozy Christmas
- Crazy About Christmas
- Dear Santa, Here's some cookies, take my brother and leave the gifts
- Dear Santa, I want it all and I want it now!
- Deck the Halls
- Don't peek, don't sneak, til' Christmas
- Down the Chimney He Came
- Elf Magic
- Enjoying the Holly days.
- Even when it's cold outside our memories keep us warm
- Everyone's a Kid at Christmas

- Faith, Hope & Love
- Families are a special part of Christmas
- Family and Friends are the True Gifts of Christmas!
- Festival of Lights
- Festive Trimmings All Merry and Bright
- Follow the star, He knows where you are.
- For Goodness Sake
- Friends and Family, that's the meaning of Christmas
- Frosty and Friends
- Gingerbread Boys!
- Girls and Boys love Toyland
- Giving feels even better than receiving
- Glad tidings we bring
- Handmade by elves
- Happy Birthday Jesus
- Happy Holidays
- Happy Holly-Days
- Happy Winter!
- Hark the Herald Angels Sing
- Have a "beary" merry Christmas!
- Have a Holly Jolly Christmas
- Have a twinkle, jingle, ringy ding Christmas
- Have yourself a beary little Christmas
- Have Yourself a Merry Little Christmas
- Here comes Santa Claus
- Here we go a caroling, a caroling we go
- Here's the scoop.. Naughty will get you nothing but poop
- He's making a list...
- He's the Reason for the Season
- HO, HO, HO
- Ho, Ho, Ho, to you
- Holiday Delights

* Holiday Goodies
* Holiday Happiness
* Holiday Hustle & Bustle
* Holiday memories warm even the coldest of days!
* Holiday Trimmings
* Holly Days
* Holly Jolly Christmas
* Home for the Holidays
* Home is the Heart of Christmas
* Home is the heart of the holidays (Christmas)
* Homespun Christmas
* How much longer must we wait? Please, Santa don't be late!
* How the Grinch Stole Christmas
* Humbugs get coal
* I Believe
* I believe in Santa.
* I can "bearly" wait for Christmas
* I love thee, Lord Jesus
* I saw Mommy kissing Santa Claus
* I wish it could be Christmas forever
* I'll Be Home for Christmas
* I'm Dreaming of a White Christmas
* In search of the perfect Tree
* It Came Upon A Midnight Clear
* It's Beginning to Look a Lot Like Christmas
* It's Christmas Time in the City
* It's in the Bag
* It's the most wonderful time of the year
* I've been good
* I've Been Really Good
* Jingle Bells

- Jesus is the heart of Christmas!
- Jesus is the reason for the season
- Jingle Bell Rock
- Jolly Holidays
- Jolly Old St. Nicholas
- Joy to the World
- Just for Santa
- Keep Christmas in our hearts forever
- Keep the spirit of Christmas through out the year
- Laughing All the Way
- Let It Glow, Let It Glow, Let It Glow
- Let It Snow, Let It Snow, Let It Snow!
- Let's meet under the mistletoe
- Lighting the Tree
- Little Santa/s
- Little Town of Bethlehem
- Little Treasures
- Look What I Got
- Love is the light of Christmas
- Love is what's in the room with you at Christmas if you stop opening presents and listen.
- Magical Christmas
- Magical Holidays
- Making a New Friend (snowman pics)
- Making Spirits Bright
- May all your Christmases be true
- May our Christmas cheer last throughout the year
- May your days be merry and bright
- Memories of the Holidays
- Meowy Christmas
- Merry and Bright
- Merry Chris Moose
- Merry Christmas
- Merry Kiss Moose

* * * * * * * * * * * * * * * * * *

- Merry Kissmiss
- Mistletoads
- Mistletoe Magic
- Moo-ey Christmas
- Must Be Santa
- Merry Christmas to all and to all a good night
- Naughty or Nice
- 'Neath the Wreath
- No matter what I get for Christmas you're all I really need.
- No place like home for the holidays
- Noel
- Oh Christmas Tree
- Oh Come All Ye Faithful
- Oh Holy Night
- Once upon a Starry Night
- Ornament Extravaganza
- Our Little Christmas Angels
- Our Snow Angel(s)
- Peace on Earth
- Presents and Carols and Lights... Oh My!
- Presents Galore
- Reindeer Crossing
- Reindeer Games
- Remember the reason for the season.
- Ring the bells! It's Christmas!
- Rockin' around the Christmas tree
- Saint Nick
- Santa Claus is Coming
- Santa stops here
- Seasons Greetings
- Seasons Meetings
- Show me the presents
- Sing Noel
- Snowman's prayer: Let it snow, let it snow, let it freeze!
- Storybook Christmas

* The Best Christmas Pageant Ever
* The best gift at Christmas is Jesus
* The Best Gift of All
* The best gift of all is family, one and all
* The best present wrapped is you with your arms around me
* The Greatest Story Ever Told
* The Grinch
* The Light Show
* The Magic of Christmas
* The Most Wonderful Time of the Year
* The Night Before Christmas
* The Nightmare Before Christmas
* The North Pole
* The Nutcracker's Sweet
* The ornaments of our home are the friends
* that gather there.
* The Perfect Tree
* The Reason for the Season
* The round man is coming to town!
* The Sights & Sounds of Christmas
* The Stockings Were Hung
* There's no people like snow people
* 'Tis the Season
* To Gramma's House We Go
* To the Spirit of Christmases past, present and future
* Too Precious for Coal
* Tree Lighting
* Trimming the Tree
* 'Twas the Night Before Christmas
* Twinkle, Sparkle Christmas Star

- Under the Tree
- Under Wraps
- Very Cool Yule
- Visions of Sugar Plums
- We Believe
- We Believe in Santa
- We break for reindeer
- White Christmas

🌲 Let's dance and sing and make good cheer, for Christmas comes but once a year. - G. MacFarren

🌲 God grant you... the belief in Christmas, which is truth; the all of Christmas, which is Christ. - Wilda English

🌲 The most vivid memories of Christmases past are usually not of gifts given or received, but of the spirit of love, the special warmth of Christmas worship, the cherished little habits of home. - Lois Rand

🌲 For unto us a child is born, unto us a son is given... his name will be called Wonderful Counselor; Mighty God, Everlasting Father; Prince of Peace. -Isaiah 9:6

🌲 Great little One! whose all-embracing birth Lifts Earth to Heaven, stoops Heaven to Earth. -Richard Crashaw

🌲 In the hearts of all children, Christmas is about family and love. –Linda LaTourelle

CHRISTMAS TREASURES

I count my treasures o'er with care,-
The little toy my darling knew,
A little sock of faded hue,
A little lock of golden hair.

Long years ago this holy time,
My little one—my all to me
Sat robed in white upon my knee,
And heard the merry Christmas chime.

"Tell me, my little golden-head,
If Santa Claus should come to-night,
What shall he bring my baby bright,--
What treasure for my boy?" I said.

And then he named this little toy,
While in his round and mournful eyes
There came a look of sweet surprise,
That spake his quiet, trustful joy.

And as he lisped his evening prayer
He asked the boon with childish grace;
Then, toddling to the chimney-place,
He hung this little stocking there.
-Eugene Fields

We're Having a twinkle, jingle, ringy ding ding Christmas

That's All I Want For Christmas

While I was out Christmas shopping
looking in all the stores around me,
I saw a small child staring at the toys.
She asked me these questions solemnly:
"Does Santa visit all the girls and boys?
Does he know their right addresses,
ones he never ever will lose?
Does he know what's right for every child
even before they get to choose?
Does he really know if they have been
bad or good or even in between?
Does he see them with a video camera
or watch them on a television screen?
Do the elves live there in Toyland,
with Santa and the Mrs. Claus?
What does he feed all the reindeer?
Do reindeer make a lot of noise?
Do you think the elves like snowballs,
and have big ole snowball fights?
Do you think that the North Pole
lies somewhere near the Northern lights?
Does Santa drink lots of hot chocolate
with big marshmallows floating on top?
Does he eat all of those cookies
that he gets at each and every stop?
Does Santa Claus have any children?
Would he like to have a little girl?
Well, he's all that I want for Christmas
more than anything else in the world!
-Lottie Ann Knox © (See Bio)

189

● ● ● ● ● ● ● ● ● ● ● ● ● ● ● ● ● ●

I'm a little snowman white and fat
I can wear a scarf or even a hat
My eyes are shiny and my nose may be too long
However they make me really isn't wrong
I love to stand and glisten in the sun
But when it gets too hot, oh,
no. I'll be gone! -Linda LaTourelle ©

Christmas Eve

Going to Grandparent's
for Christmas Eve
Is something we love to do

We enjoy the visit
on Christmas Eve
And look forward to it
all year through!
Grandma and Grandpa
Love us so much
They kiss our cheeks and
Our faces they touch
We love to open gifts
And their beautiful tree
Is always a delightful

And wonderful sight to see.
But this by far
The most wonderful part
They listen to us
From the depth of their hearts!
Thena Smith © (See Bio)

Ho, Ho
Ho!

Gingerbread Man Recipe for Life

1 heaping cup of Encouragement
1 cup melted Compassion
2 cups Hope
1 cup Love
2 tbsp. Faith
(it only takes a little)
2 large Attitude
Hugs
in assorted sizes

Cream encouragement and compassion together. Add hope, love and faith. Mix thoroughly until smooth. Slowly add the unbeaten attitude. Batter should be smooth but not unyielding. Knead gently. Roll in hugs and cut to the desired shape. Add stars for eyes and a kiss on the mouth. Bake in a warm oven. Excellent when shared with a child.   -Unknown

TWAS THE NIGHT BEFORE
CHRISTMAS

'Twas the night before Christmas, when all through the house...not a creature was stirring, not even a mouse. The stockings were hung by the chimney with care, in hopes that St Nicholas soon would be there. The children were nestled all snug in their beds, while visions of sugar plums danced in their heads...

-Clement C. Moore

I saw Baby kissing Daddy underneath the mistletoe

Away in a manger...
the little Lord Jesus lay down his
sweet head

Have yourself a
Merry Little Christmas
Baby Dear

Merry Christmas to all and to all a goodnight!

Easter

Jesus Lives
He Live for you
And me
He rose again
To set us free

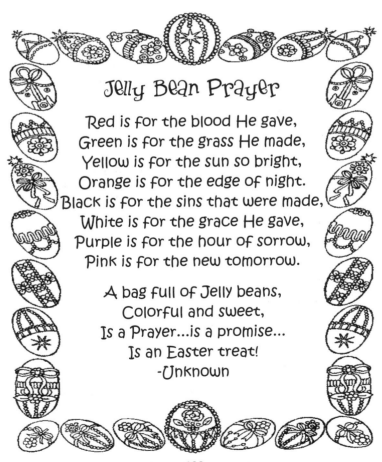

Jelly Bean Prayer

Red is for the blood He gave,
Green is for the grass He made,
Yellow is for the sun so bright,
Orange is for the edge of night.
Black is for the sins that were made,
White is for the grace He gave,
Purple is for the hour of sorrow,
Pink is for the new tomorrow.

A bag full of Jelly beans,
Colorful and sweet,
Is a Prayer...is a promise...
Is an Easter treat!
-Unknown

193

• • • • • • • • • • • • • • • • •

The Easter Bunny

There's a story quite funny,
About a toy bunny,
And the wonderful things she can do;
Every bright Easter morning,
Without warning,
She colors eggs, red, green, or blue.

Some she covers with spots,
Some with quaint little dots,
And some with strange mixed colors, too
-- Red and green, blue and yellow,
But each unlike his fellow
Are eggs of every hue.

And it's odd, as folks say,
That on no other day
In all of the whole year through,
Does this wonderful bunny,
So busy and funny,
Color eggs of every hue.

If this story you doubt
She will soon find you out,
And what do you think she will do?
On the next Easter morning
She'll bring you without warning,
Those eggs of every hue.
-M. Josephine Todd, 1909

Here comes Peter Cottontail
Hoppin' down the bunny trail
Bringing lots of joy for Baby dear

Easter

- He is Risen
- A hunting we will go...
- A 24 Carrot day
- A basket full of goodies
- A hunting we will go..
- A tisket, A tasket
- A tisket, a tasket, I found my Easter basket
- A very bunny
- An egg-citing resurrection story
- An eggs-stra special Easter
- Baskets and bunnies
- Baskets of Fun
- Coloring eggs
- Easter bonnet
- Easter egg morning
- Easter egg-citement
- Easter morn
- Easter parade
- Easter Poohrade
- Easter-ific
- Easter's on its way
- Egg painting zone
- Egg-cited for Easter
- Eggstravaganza
- Funny bunny
- Get crackin'
- Happy Easter
- Have a sp'egg'tacular Eater
- Here comes Peter Cottontail
- Hippity Hoppity Hooray
- Hippity..Hoppity
- Hippity... Hoppity Easter's on its way
- Hopping down the bunny trail
- Hoppy Easter
- Hunting Egggs
- I'm Egg-stra special
- In my easter bonnet
- In your Easter bonnet
- One cute Easter Chick
- Some Bunny Loves me
- Sp'egg'tacular Easter
- Snuggle bunny
- The easter bunny came!

195

Halloween

Trick or Treaters

They all come knock on the door,
And just stand there waiting.
While their small energies soar,
Their thoughts are anticipating
On what great goody will they get/
What tasty wrapped treat will whet
Their young hungry budding appetites
On this October night of all nights?
Someone opens up the door to greet them,
Amid the shouts of 'Trick or Treat!'
I see: ghosts, goblins, ghouls, and bats
Skeletons, babies, ladies, dogs, and jaws,
Hobos, cowboys, M&Ms, and Santa Clause
Witches, pumpkins, Snow White and a cop.
Just when does this colorful parade stop?
Slowly their hurrying footsteps lag.
Their hands, holding a heavy bulging bag.
Tonight has been one terrific Scream!
Scary, Wacky, Weird, & Fun Halloween!
-Lottie Knox

Halloween time is here again,
time to play Trick or Treat.
Pumpkin time is here again,
our spooky friends we'll meet.

Halloween Titles

- A bootiful night
- A "spooktacular" event
- A monstrously good kid
- Batty over Halloween
- Beary Scary
- Bobbing for apples
- Boo to you!
- Broom parking 5¢
- Carving out memories
- Come as you aren't
- Costume crazy
- Costume parade
- Costumes and pumpkins and candy, oh my!
- Count your blessings
- Creatures of the night
- Creepy cat
- Creepy characters
- Creepy crawler
- Cutest little pumpkin in the patch
- Disguise the limit
- Don't be scared...it's just us
- Frightfully Delightful
- Gather a harvest of love
- Getting into the spirit of Halloween
- Guess who
- Halloween Howls
- Halloween is a real treat
- Happy Pumpkin day
- Happy spook day
- Happy trick or treating
- Howl-O-Ween
- I am the treat!
- I'm a pleasing pumkin
- In search of the perfect pumpkin
- It's pumpkin time!
- It's the great pumkin Charlie Brown!
- Jeepers Creepers
- Just a little bit corny
- Just say boo
- Master of disguises
- Mommy's lil' pumpkins
- Mommy's lil' monsters
- Monster mash
- Will spook for treats
- Yum, Yum, give me some

July 4th

- ☆ America, We Salute You
- ☆ Little Patriot
- ☆ Red, White And Blue, Through And Through
- ☆ The American Spirit
- ☆ United We Stand
- ☆ All decked out in red, white and blue
- ☆ America the Beautiful
- ☆ American Made
- ☆ Born in the USA
- ☆ Celebrating the 4th
- ☆ Diamonds in the Sky
- ☆ Fireworks Fun
- ☆ God Bless America
- ☆ A Grand Old Flag
- ☆ Hurray for the red, white and blue
- ☆ I Love the USA
- ☆ Independence Day
- ☆ KaBoom time

- ☆ Little Patriot
- ☆ My All American Baby
- ☆ Old Glory
- ☆ Pint-sized Patriot
- ☆ A Sparkling Good Time
- ☆ Sweet Land of Liberty
- ☆ Star Spangled Banner
- ☆ Stars & Stripes Forever
- ☆ Sweet Land of Liberty
- ☆ This land is your land
- ☆ Yankee Doodle Dandy
- ☆ You're a grand old flag, you're a high flying flag

A ROCKET IN MY POCKET

I've got a rocket in my pocket; I cannot stop to play. Away it goes! I've burned my toes. It's Independence Day

198

Red, white, and blue
Flying for liberty
Flying for children here
Flying for peace everywhere
It's a symbol of all that's true
It's the best for me and you
The grand old flag of freed

God bless America
Land that I love
Stand beside her
And guide her,
Through the
night
With the light
From above.

Old Glory

My red is deeper,
for the blood
you've shed.
My white is purer,
for your pain.
My blue will be bluer
than the deepest sea
when you come home again.

My country, 'tis of thee,
Sweet land of liberty,
Of thee I sing;
Land where my fathers died,
Land of the pilgrims' pride,
From every mountainside,
Let freedom ring

Born in the

U.S.A.

St. Patricks Day

- ♣ A little bit of blarney
- ♣ A reluctant Leprechaun
- ♣ Blarney spoken here
- ♣ Feelin' green
- ♣ For love of Ireland
- ♣ Happy St. Paddy's Day
- ♣ Irish Blessings
- ♣ Irish lassie
- ♣ Irish eyes
- ♣ Irish princess
- ♣ It's not that easy being green
- ♣ Looking for Leprechauns
- ♣ Luck of the Irish
- ♣ Lucky Charmers
- ♣ Lucky four-leaf clover
- ♣ Lucky me

- ♣ Our little Leprechaun
- ♣ Our pot of gold
- ♣ Pretty Irish girl
- ♣ The end of the rainbow
- ♣ The pipes are calling
- ♣ The wearin of the Green
- ♣ When Irish eyes are smiling

May God watch you every night, may your days be clear and bright. My God smile on all you do. May you always to His love be true.

200

Thanksgiving

- Be ye thankful
- Bless this Food
- Bunch of Turkeys
- Carving memories
- Count your blessings
- A Day of Thanks
- Family Traditions
- The Feast
- Give thanks
- Gobble! Gobble!
- God is Great...God is Good
- I'm thankful for...
- In Everything Give Thanks
- It's Turkey Time!
- Nap Time
- Pumpkin Pie
- True Family Gathering

Over the river and through the wood,
To Grandfather's house we go;
The horse knows the way
To carry the sleigh
Through the white and drifted snow.
Over the river and through the wood
Trot fast, my dapple-gray!
Spring over the ground,
Like a hunting-hound!
For this is Thanksgiving Day.
Over the river and through the wood -
Now Grandmother's cap I spy!
Hurrah for the fun!
"Is the pudding done?
Hurrah for the pumpkin-pie!"
-Lydia Child

Thank you for the earth and sky.
Thank you for the bids that fly.
Thank you for the food we grow.
Thank you for the streams that flow.
Thanks you, thank you; this we say.
Thanks for all we have today!

Turkey Dinner, Turkey Dinner
Gather round, gather round
Who will eat the drumstick
Yummy, yummy drumstick
All sit down, all sit down

Little Pilgrim dressed in gray
on that first Thanksgiving Day.
Little Indian dressed in brown,
Came to visit Plymouth Town,
They both came to eat and pray
on that first Thanksgiving Day.
Hello, Mr. Turkey how are you?
His feet go wobble, wobble
And his head goes Gobble, Gobble.
Hello, Mr. Turkey, how are you?

Thanksgiving time is here
Let's give a great big cheer
For food and friends and family
Thanksgiving time is here.

I'm a little turkey
Short and Fat
Thanksgiving Day is coming
Now what do you think of that?
I had better run as fast as I can
Or your mommy will roast me in a pan!

Five fat turkeys sitting on a fence
The first one said," Oh, my am I immense!"
The second one said, "I can gobble at you"
The third one said, " I can gobble too"
The fourth one said, ""I can spread my tail"
The fifth one said, "Don't catch it on a nail"
The farmer came by and had to say,
"Turkeys look best on Thanksgiving Day!"

I eat Turkey,
I eat Turkey.
Yes, I do
Yes, I do
Turkey in my tummy,
Yummy, yummy, yummy.
Good for me
Good for you.

Gobble, gobble turkey talk,
Turkeys all around,
Standing up and sitting down,
Turkeys on the ground.

Lord, we thank thee for this food,
Bless it to our bodies God.
Help us live Thy name to praise,
Serving thee, through all our days.

Valentine's Day

- Valentines
- A friend Hugs my Heart
- Friend to Friend, Heart to Heart
- Friendship is the thread that ties all Heart together.
- Friendship warms the Heart
- Loving Hearts bloom
- Grandmas' Little Heart throbs Grandkids keep Hearts young.
- The joy of grandchildren is measured in the Heart.
- A mother holds her children's hand for a while, their Hearts forever
- A mother's love is the Heart of the home.
- Families are tied together with Heartstrings.

Here's a special card for you,
Will you please be mine?
It's filled with hugs and lots of love,
Be my valentine!

Hugs and kisses
Hugs and kisses, I love you.
Hugs and kisses,
Hugs and kisses for you.

You're a special
Baby of mine
Baby of mine
Baby of mine
You're a special
Baby of mine
Be my valentine!

I've got a big red heart
That I will give to you.
It brings you love and kisses,
Because you are my Baby.

Valentine's Day

- ♡ 100% Lovable
- ♡ 4 My Love
- ♡ Be Mine
- ♡ Be my Cupid
- ♡ Be My Love
- ♡ Be My Sweetie
- ♡ Be My Valentine
- ♡ Bunches of Love
- ♡ Call Me Cupid
- ♡ Love is in the air
- ♡ Candy Kisses
- ♡ Circle of Love
- ♡ Cupid's Cuties
- ♡ Cupid's Kisses
- ♡ Forever Yours
- ♡ I love your funny face
- ♡ Gimme a Kiss
- ♡ Happy Valentine's Day
- ♡ Heart of my Heart
- ♡ Hearts and Kisses
- ♡ Heartthrob!
- ♡ How do I love thee...
- ♡ How Sweet it Is
- ♡ Hugs and Kisses!
- ♡ Prince Charming
- ♡ Let Me Call You Sweetheart
- ♡ Love Bugs
- ♡ Love Me Tender
- ♡ Love Notes
- ♡ Loves Me...Loves Me Not
- ♡ My Funny Valentine
- ♡ My Girl
- ♡ Only You
- ♡ Perfect Valentine
- ♡ Sealed with a Kiss
- ♡ The Sweetest Days
- ♡ V is for Valentine
- ♡ Be My Valentine?
- ♡ XOXOXOXOX
- ♡ You Belong to Me

• • • • • • • • • • • • • • • • •

HUGS AND KISSES

KISS AND MAKE IT WELL

I sit at my window and sew and dream,
While my little boy at play
Bewails my thoughts from hem and seam
As he frolics the livelong day;
But time and again he comes to me
With a sorrowful tale to tell,
And mother must look at the scratch or bump,
Then kiss it and make it well.

So I kiss head, and his knee, and his arm,
And the dear little grimy hand;
And who can fathom the magic charm,
And who can understand?
For I even kiss when he bites his tongue,
And love works its mystic spell,
For there's never a cut, nor a scratch, nor a bump,
But mother can kiss it well

'Tis a foolish whim, do you say? Ah, yes!
But the foolish things of earth
Have taught the wise, since a little child
In Bethlehem had his birth.
And we know that many an older hear—
We know, but we do not tell—
Will never be free from its bitter smart
Till kisses have made it well.

Kisses full of sugar and hug sublime
Oh, what a wonderful child of mine

Mama's Kisses

A kiss when I wake in the morning,
A kiss when I go to bed,
A kiss when I burn my fingers,
A kiss when I bump my head;

A kiss when my bath is over,
A kiss when my bath begins;
My mamma is as full of kisses
As full as nurse is of pins.

Bear Hugs & Kangaroo Kisses

⊛ 100% Huggable.

⊛ A grandma/grandpa is a hug waiting to happen

⊛ A hug a day keeps the grumpys away

⊛ A Hug a Day keeps the Monsters Away

⊛ A hug in the heart gives each day a fresh start

⊛ A hug is a gift that warms the heart

⊛ A hug is a great gift...one size fits all...and it's easy to exchange.

⊛ A hug is a handshake from the heart.

⊛ A hug is a roundabout way of expressing affection

⊛ A hug is the shortest distance between friends.

⊛ A hug makes my day

⊛ A Kiss for Luck

⊛ A kiss is a jumper cable of the heart

⊛ A kiss is a secret told to the mouth instead of the ear.

⊛ As you read this know that I am sending you a warm hug

Hugging

♡ Children are for hugging

♡ Cookies and hugs make life bearable

♡ Babies are a Special Hug From God!

♡ Gimme a Kiss, will ya?

♡ Handle with hugs

♡ Huggable, lovable you

♡ Hugging closes the door to hate. Kissing opens the door to love.

♡ Huggly, buggly, I love to snuggly

♡ Hugs and kisses, stars for wishes

♡ Hugs are beary special

♡ Hugs given here.

♡ Hugs and love

♡ Huggy bug

♡ Hugs to You.

♡ If a hug represented how much I loved you, I would hold you in my arms forever.

♡ I wish I was a teddy bear, everybody loves them, nobody cares if they're fat and the older they get the more cuddly they become.

♡ Millions and millions of years would still not give me half enough time to describe that moment of eternity I feel when I hug you.

♡ Mom makes hugs happen

♡ My favorite place to be is inside of your hugs where it's warm and loving.

♡ Sealed with a Kiss

♡ Smooch

♡ The soul that can speak through the eyes can also kiss with a gaze. - Becquer

♡ This hug's for you!

HUMOR

- Never trust a dog to watch your food

- When you want something expensive, ask your grandparents.

- Never tell your little brother that you're not going to do what your mother told you to do.

- Don't' pick on your sister when she's holding a baseball bat.

- When your Dad is mad and asks you, "Do I look stupid?" Don't answer him.

- Children seldom misquote you. In fact, they usually repeat word for word what you shouldn't have said.

- Insanity is hereditary, you usually get it from your kids.

- Children are natural mimics who act like their parents, despite every effort to teach them good manners.

- Getting six hours of sleep is a privilege.

- Giving birth is like taking your lower lip and forcing it over your head. –Carol Burnett

- First you teach a child to talk, then you teach him to be quiet.

Children are the hands by which we take hold of heaven.

-MHenry Ward Beecher

⊛ Any child will tell you that he sole purpose for a middle name is so he can tell when he's in trouble.

⊛ A baby is a kiss factory. No matter how many kisses you steal they still have an abundant supply.

⊛ A baby is hope and love and joy!

⊛ Flowers are words which even a baby can understand. ─Arthur C. Coxe

⊛ Children are the only form of immortality that we can be sure of. ─Peater Ustinov

⊛ Trust yourself. You know more than you think you do. -Dr. Benjamin Spock

⊛ A mother's children are portraits of herself.

⊛ Children need love especially when they don't deserve it.

⊛ Children are our future...treat them well or they'll remind you about it in your old age.

⊛ Children are the answer, what was the question?

⊛ If evolution really works, how come mothers only have two hands? -Milton Berle

⊛ It is not economical to go to bed early to save the candles if the result is twins.

⊛ Raising kids is part joy and part guerilla warfare.

Jelly Fish

THE JELLY FISH

The Jelly fish- it has no skeleton.
it's just a glob of living gelatin.
Another thing about that glob gelatinous:
It's as flat as we'd be if an elephant sat on us.
And though it sometimes shines and shimmers,
no one likes it - especially swimmers.
It's not the Jello-y part we mind
but those nasty tentacles that trail behind.
So Jellyfish, Jellyfish, here's my prayer:
When I go swimming, I hope you're not there.
-Joe Thompson © (See Bio)

Jump Rope Rhymes

Say, Say my playmate
Come out and play with me
and bring your dollies 3
Climb up my apple tree
slide down my rain barrel
into my cellar door
and we'll be jolly friends
forever more - more - more !

Jump Rope Rhymes

A sailor went to sea, sea, sea. To see what he could
see, see, see. But all that he could see, see,
see. Was the bottom of the deep blue sea, sea, sea.

Blue bells, cockle shell
Easy ivy over

Apples, peaches, pears and plums
Tell me when your birthday comes.

Cinderella, dressed in yellow
went upstairs to kiss a 'fella
made a mistake
and kissed a snake
how many doctors
did it take?

Down in the valley where the green grass grows,
There sat _____, as pretty as a rose.
She sang high, she sang sweet,
Along came _____ and kissed her on the
cheek.
How many kisses did she get?
1, 2, 3, 4, 5, 6....

Lullaby

Jolles Lullaby

Soft little cuddly one go to sleep
Wee Willy Winkle's come, dimple your cheeks
Sandman is ready to sprinkle your dreams
With white velvet lambs in pastures of green
Lambs are a-jumpin', one hundred and one
Ponies are playing out under the sun
Lilies and ladybugs sway in the breeze
Flowers and butterflies cover the trees
Dimple your cheeks, dear, and close your eyes
Sandman has come with a big surprise
Gifts from the fairy queen dusted with gold
Love from your mommy and daddy who hold
You softly -Laurie Conable © (See Bio)

I hear thy voice, dear Lord;
I hear it by the stormy sea
When winter nights are
black and wild,
And when, affright,
I call to Thee;
It calms my fears
and whispers me,
"Sleep well, my child."

CRADLE SONG

We will go sailing, my girlie and I,
To the summer land,
To the summer land,
Where are roses and robins, and butterflies gay,
And the little brooks that do nothing but play,
And sugar and honey, and cinnamon spice,
And candy and almonds and everything nice.
We would like to anchor awhile and stay;
But we must go sailing, away, away,
While the waters are smooth and the sky is bright,
For baby and I must be home to-night.
So on we go sailing, my girlie and I,
To the winter land,
Where the snow is as white as white can be,
And diamonds and pearls hang from every tree;
Where the wood fires blaze up clear and bright,
And Santa clause comes, every Christmas night.
But we must go sailing, away, away;
There's a storm coming on, and the wind is high,
And we must get home, my girlie and I.
So now we sail homeward, my girlie and I,
To the land of Nod,
To the land Nod.
Roses and spices are very sweet,
And candy and honey are good to eat,
And diamonds and pearls are pretty to wear;
But what does a tired little girl care,
But to cuddle down on her mother's breast,
And go to sleep like a bird in its nest.
For there's never a land beneath sun or star
That's so sweet as the land where the mammas are.

Hushaby, My Own

Fair is the castle on the hill
Hushaby, sweet my own!
The night is fair, and the waves are still.
And the wind is singing to you and to me
In this lowly home beside the sea
Hushaby, sweet my own!
-Eugene Fields

All the Pretty Little Horses

Hush a bye, don't you cry,
Go to sleep ye little baby.
When you wake, you shall take
All the pretty little horses.
Blacks and grays, dapples and bays
Coach and six little horses,
Blacks and grays, dapples and bays,
Coach and six little horses.
Hush a bye, don't you cry,
Go to sleep ye little baby...

Sweet dreams my child
Dear baby of mine
Sweet dreams

THE ROCK-A-BY LADY

The Rock-a-By Lady from Hushaby street
Comes stealing, comes creeping;
The poppies they hang from her head to her feet,
And each hath a dream that is tiny and fleet—
She bringeth her poppies to you, my sweet,
When she findeth you sleeping!

There is one little dream of a beautiful drum—
"Rub-a-dub!" it goeth;
There is one little dream of a big sugar-plum,
And lo! Thick and fast the other dreams come
Of popguns that band, and tin tops that hum,
And a trumpet that bloweth!

And dollies peep out of those wee little dreams
With laughter and singing;
And boats go a-floating on silvery streams,
And the stars peek-a-boo with their own misty gleams
and up, up, and up, where the Mother Moon beams,
the fairies go winging!

Would you dream all these dreams that are tiny and fleet?
They'll come to you sleeping;
So shut the two eyes that are weary, my sweet,
For the Rock-a-By Lady from Hushaby street,
With poppies that hang from her head to her feet,
Comes stealing; comes creeping.

-Eugene Field

Hushaby darling mother is here
Holding you close and ever so near
Sleep little child in my arms full of love
Knowing that Jesus is protecting above

-Linda LaTourelle

JEWISH LULLABY

My harp is on the willow-tree,
Else would I sing, O love, to thee
A song of long-ago—
Perchance the song that Miriam sung
Ere yet Judea's heart was wrung
By centuries of woe.

I ate my crest in tears to-day,
As scourged I went upon my way—
And yet my darling smiled;
Aye, beating at my breast, he laughed—
My anguish curdled not the draught—
'Twas sweet with love, my child!

The shadow of the centuries lies
Deep in thy dark and mournful eyes;
But, hush! and close them now,
And in the dreams that thou shalt dream
The light of other days shall seem
To glorify they brow!

Our harp is on the willow-tree—
I have no song to sing to thee,
As shadows round us roll;
But, hush and sleep, and thou shalt hear
Jehovah's voice that speaks to cheer
Judea's fainting soul!
-Eugene Field

Now then sleep, sleep my child.
Sleep and dream my lovely child.

SWEET AND LOW

Sleep and rest, sleep and rest,
Father will come to thee soon;
Rest, rest, on mother's breast,
Father will come to thee soon;
Father will come
to his babe in the nest,
Silver sails all out of the west
Under the silver moon:
Sleep, my little one,
sleep, my pretty one, sleep.
-Alfred Tennyson

Sleep my little babe
Sleep my precious soul;
Sleep all through the night
My little morning star.

BED IS TOO SMALL

Bed is too small for my tiredness.
Give me a hilltop of trees.
Tuck a cloud up under my chin.
Lord, blow the moon out, please.
Rock me to sleep in a cradle of dreams,
Sing me a lullabye of leaves.
Tuck a cloud up under my chin,
Lord, blow the moon out, please.

Hush Little Child

Hush little child,
whimpering in dreams
your all cosy and warm,
wrapped in rainbows and moonbeams
outside the wind howls,
there's frost on the ground
And Autumn is whining,
its early warning sound
so hush my baby,
there's no cause for alarm
for in your life,
you'll face many a storm
But with God at your side,
there is nothing to fear
Because his love and affection,
will always be near.

-Michael Levy © (See Bio)

Do you ever sing your own lullaby?
Lullabies can bring such special memories and
feelings of a wonderful time in our life. A time
of peaceful togetherness resting in love.

Cry Baby Bunting
Daddy's gone a-hunting
Gone to fetch a rabbit skin
To wrap the Baby Bunting in
Cry Baby Bunting

♡

Sleep, baby, sleep,
Thy papa guards the sheep;
Thy mama shakes the dreamland tree
And from it fall sweet dreams for thee,
Sleep, baby, sleep,
Sleep, baby, sleep,
Our cottage vale is deep;
The little lamb is on the green,
With woolly fleece so soft and clean,
Sleep, baby, sleep,
Sleep, baby, sleep,
Down where the woodbines creep;
Be always like the lamb so mild,
A kind and sweet and gentle child

Rock-a-by baby
on the tree top
When the wind blows
the cradle will rock

Bedtime Treats

Bedtime treats
Are little bare feet,
Kisses upon the head,
Lullabies, closing eyes,
Prayers beside the bed.
Bedtime treats
Are stories and songs,
The moon casting shadows on the wall,
Don't let the bed bugs bite,
Hold me tight and
Nightlights in the hall.
Bedtime Treats
Are recapturing the day
An "I love you" before you go,
Closing the door, with the hpe
They'll be more,
How can we ever know.
-Shanda Purcell©

Rock-a-by me Jesus

Hush Little Baby

Hush, little baby, don't say a word,
Mama's going to buy you a mockingbird.
And if that mockingbird don't sing,
Mama's going to buy you a diamond ring.
And if that diamond ring turns brass,
Mama's going to buy you a looking glass.
And if that looking glass gets broke,
Mama's going to buy you a billy goat.
And if that billy goat won't pull,
Mama's going to buy you a cart and bull.
And if that cart and bull turn over,
Mama's going to buy you a dog named Rover.
And if that dog named Rover won't bark,
Mama's going to buy you a horse and cart.
And if that horse and cart fall down,
You'll still be the sweetest little baby in town.

Thee I love, sweetest dove,
Darling little baby!
While I live, thee I'll give
Kisses warm as may be.

• • • • • • • • • • • • • • • • • •

Winken, Blinken and Nod

Winken, Blinken, and Nod one night
Sailed off in a wooden shoe
Sailed off on a river of crystal light,
Into a sea of dew.
"Where are you going,
and what do you wish?"
The old moon asked the three.
"We have come to fish
for the herring fish
That live in the beautiful sea;
Nets of silver and gold have we!"
Said Winken, Blinken, and Nod.
The old moon laughed and sang a song,
As they rocked in the wooden shoe,
And the wind that sped them all night long
Ruffled the waves of dew.
The little stars were the herring fish
That lived in the beautiful sea
"Now cast your nets wherever you wish
Never afeard are we";
So cried the stars to the fisherman three:
Winken, Blinken, and Nod.

-continued

-continued

All night long their nets they threw
To the stars in the twinkling foam
Then down from the skies came the wooden shoe
Bringing the fisherman home;
'Twas all so pretty a sail it seemed
As if it could not be,
And some folks thought 'twas
a dream they'd dreamed
Of sailing that beautiful sea
But I shall name you the fishermen three:
Winken, Blinken, and Nod.
Winken and Blinken are two little eyes,
And Nod is a little head,
And the wooden shoes that sailed the skies
Is the wee one's trundle-bed.
So shut your eyes while mother sings
Of wonderful sights that be,
And you shall see the beautiful things
As you rock in the misty sea,
Where the old shoe rocked
hte fisherman three:
Winken, Blinken, and Nod.

Nighty-Night

Good night, sleep tight,
Wake up bright
In the morning light
Sweet dreams
For you are loved
And safe from God above.
-Eugene Field

All Through The Night

Sleep, my child and peace attend thee
All through the night;
Guardian angels God will send thee,
All through the night.
Soft the drowsy hours are creeping
Hill and vale in slumber steeping,
I my loving vigil keeping
All through the night.

♡

Lullaby and good night, with pink roses bedight
With lilies o'er spread is my baby's wee bed
Lay thee down now and rest, may thy slumber be blessed
Lay thee down now and rest, may thy slumber be blessed

♡

Sleep sound in Jesus
He will keep you in love
His Father is watching
From Heaven above

Lullaby, and Good Night

Ver. 1

Lullaby and good night,
In the sky stars are bright,
while roses in bloom,
Fill with fragrance the room.
With the morning, if God will,
You will waken again;
With the morn, if God will,
You will waken again.
Lullaby, have no fear,
Guardian angels are near,
Their watch they will keep,
While children go to sleep.
Dream the dark night away,
Till God's sun brings the day;
Dream the dark night away,
Till God's sun brings the day.

Toora, loora, loora
Toora, loora, li
Sleep Baby Sleep
Toora, loora, li

Lullaby, and Good Night
Ver. 2

Lullaby, and good night,
You're your mother's delight,
Shining angels beside
My darling abide.
Soft and warm is your bed,
Close your eyes and rest your head.
Soft and warm is your bed,
Close your eyes and rest your head.

Lullabye, and goodnight
in the soft evening light,
like a rose in it's bed,
lay down your sweet head.
When the morning is here,
I will wake you my dear,
when the morning is here

Lullaby and good night,
thy mother's delight
Bright angels beside
my darling abide
They will guard thee at rest,
thou shalt wake on my breast

• • • • • • • • • • • • • • • •

SO, SO, ROCK-A-BY SO!

So, so, rock-a-by so!
Off to the garden where dreamikins grow;
And here is a kiss on your winkyblink eyes,
And here is a kiss on your dimpledown cheek
And here is a kiss for the treasure that lies
In the beautiful garden way up in the skies
Which you seek.
Now mind these three kisses wherever you go
So, so, rock-a-by so!

There's one little fumfay who lives there, I know,
For he dances all night where the dreamikins grow;
I send him this kiss on your rosy red cheek.
And here is a kiss for the dram that shall rise
When the fumfay shall dance in those far-away skies
Which you seek.
Be sure that you pay those three kisses you owe
So, so, rock-a-by so!
And, by-low, as you rock-a-by go
Don't forget mother who loveth you so!
-Eugene Field

ALL THROUGH THE NIGHT

Sleep, my child and peace attend thee
All through the night;
Guardian angels God will send thee,
All through the night.
Soft the drowsy hours are creeping
Hill and vale in slumber steeping,
I my loving vigil keeping
All through the night.

Lullaby

Lullaby, oh lullaby!
Flowers are closed
and lambs are sleeping;
Lullaby, oh lullaby!
Stars are up,
the moon is peeping;
Lullaby, oh lullaby!
While the birds
are silence keeping,
Lullaby, oh lullaby!
Sleep, my baby,
fall a-sleeping,
Lullaby, oh lullaby!
-Christina Rosetti

Golden Slumbers Kiss Your Eyes

Golden slumbers kiss your eyes,
Smiles awake you when you rise.
Sleep, pretty wantons, do not cry,
And I will sing a lullaby:
Rock them, rock them, lullaby.
Care is heavy, therefore sleep you;
You are care, and care must keep you.
Sleep, pretty wantons, do not cry,
And I will sing a lullaby:
Rock them, rock them, lullaby.

The Midnight Cry

A wee soft cry in the still of the night
Calls out for a mother's touch
To soothe and calm her little one
Who yearns for the bosom so warm
Caress so gentle baby's pink cheek
And tenderly sing a sweet lullaby
In the language only a mother can speak
Whisper your love and devotion
as you rock this precious babe to sleep
-Linda LaTourelle

Hush, my dear, lie still and slumber,
Holy angels guard thy bed!
Heavenly blessings without number
Gently falling on thy head.
-Isaac Watts

I do believe that God above created you for me to love. He picked you out from all the rest, 'cause he knew I loved you best

Lullaby

❀ Lullaby, oh lullaby! Flow'rs are closed and lambs are sleeping. Lullaby, oh lullaby! While the birds are silence keeping: Lullaby, oh lullaby! Sleep, my baby, fall a-sleeping. Lullaby, oh lullaby!

❀ Sleep, pretty baby, the world awaits day with you; Morning returns to us ever too soon. Roses unfold, in their loveliness, all for you; Blossom the lilies for hope of your glance.

'Tis I that nurse the babe and rock his cradle to and fro; 'tis I that lull and lullay him, unceasingly and low. On this day's morn, alack! He cried from midnight until three; but it is I that lose my sleep, the care is all on me.

❀ Hush-a-by, don't you cry, Go to sleep, little baby. When you wake, You shall have all the pretty little horses

❀ Sleep, my baby, on my bosom, warm and cozy it will prove; Round thee mother's arms are folding. In her heart a mother's love. Sleep my darling babe in quiet, sleep on mother's gentle breast.

❀ Sweet Baby of Mine, sleep gently and rest. Forever my love you will always be blessed. My darling I love you, my baby so fair. In you is a gift so precious and rare. I cherish and adore you with all of my heart. You were our special infant right from the start.
       –LaTourelle

Sweet Dreams

NOTHING TO DO

The tower of Babel I built of blocks
Come down with a crash to the floor.
My train of cars ran over the rocks—
I'll warrant they'll run no more;

Imagination

The imagination of a child
Is a wonder to behold,
And sometimes they don't grow up,
Until they're very old.
The child within our mind
Can imagine fairy sprites,
Or make a fairy tale
Out of visions of delight.
I grew up hearing stories
And tales of make believe,
My Grandma used to hold me
On her lap as she would read.
Myth or imagination
Are what dreams are made of,
And if we teach our children,
They'll also know about God above.
God plays an important part
In my life and work,
My gift is from Him,
I'm only the scribe.
So if you see something,
That really isn't there,
Perhaps you should look inside
And see that God is everywhere.
-Sandra Prouse © (See Bio)

- Imagination is the highest kite that one can fly. - Lauren Bacall

- Imagination is more important than words -Einstein

- You cannot depend on your eyes when your imagination is out of focus. -Mark Twain

- Boredom excites imagination -Dostoevsky

- Your imagination, my dear fellow, is worth more than you imagine. -Louis Aragon

- To invent, you need a good imagination and a pile of junk. -Edison

- Many live in the ivory tower called reality; they never venture on the open sea of thought. - Francois Gautier

- If you want to build a ship, don't drum up the men to gather wood, divide the work, and give orders. Instead, teach them to yearn for the vast and endless sea. -de Saint Exubery

Dream my beautiful child of the endless possibilities that are before you. Play and learn and grow. Life is the joy you make it...with God's help, of course. -Linda LaTourelle

A Good Play

We built a ship upon the stairs
All made of the back-bedroom chairs,
And filled it full of sofa pillows
To go a-sailing on the billows.

We took a saw and several nails,
And water in the nursery pails;
And Tom said, "Let us also take
An apple and a slice of cake";--
Which was enough for Tom and me
To go a-sailing on, till tea.

We sailed along for days and days,
And had the very best of plays;
But Tom fell out and hurt his knee,
So there was no one left but me.

-Robert Louis Stevenson

If you can't believe, just make Believe!

AS I WAS GOING UP THE STAIR

As I was going up the stair
I met a man who wasn't there.
He wasn't there again today—
Oh, how I wish he'd go away.

Woo Hoo!

IF I WERE A FISH

If I could have a single wish
I'd dearly wish to be a fish
Swimming in the deep blue sea
But if I were a fish I think
I'd have no chocolate milk to drink
None of my favorite songs to sing
No playing on a tire swing
I couldn't hug my family
And I know they would surely miss me!
So though a fish's life sounds cool
I'll stick to swimming in the pool.

 Imagination is a grand thing to have

 Oh, What an Imagination!

 Welcome to the Land of Pretending, a place where joy is never ending

 Dream a little dream

MY SISTER NIAMH AND ME

We're going on an adventure
My sister Niamh and me
Cause an Indian Maharaja
Has invited us for tea
There are tigers in the jungle
And the elephants roam free
Lots of fun for both of us
My sister Niamh and me
We're going on an adventure
My sister Niamh and me
Where fleets of Spanish galleons
Are sailing on the sea
There's chests all full of treasure
And pirates one, two, three
A day with Captain Blackbeard for
My sister Niamh and me
We're going on an adventure
My sister Niamh and me
For a trip around the Milky Way
There's lots of things to see
Where spaceships fly around the stars
And the moon is made of cheese
But now it's time we went to bed
My sister Niamh and me
-Rob Erskine © (See Bio)

NOTHING TO DO

Oh my what shall I do?
There's nothing here to play.
I guess I'll read a book
And travel eons away!

Voyage in the Armchair

Oh, papa! Dear papa! We've had such a fine game!
We played at a sail on the sea;
The old arm-chair made such a beautiful ship,
And it sailed, oh, as nice as could be.
The whale was the sofa, and it, dear papa,
Is at least twice as large as our ship;
Our captain called out, "Turn the ship round about!"
Oh, I wish we had not come on this trip!
And we all cried, "Oh yes, let us get away home,
And hide in some corner quite snug;"
So, we sailed for the fireside as quick as we could,
And we landed all safe on the rug.

My Radio Flyer

It's a rocket ship
For a ride to Mars
It's a racing machine
It's the fastest of cars...
It's a stallion
only ridden by medieval knights
It's a time machine
Or a capsule for space flights.
It can do anything
That I want it to do
It just looks like
A Radio Flyer to you....

-Thena Smith ©

The Day The Pirates Came To Tea

Shiver me timbers and pieces of eight
A band of old pirates turned up at our gate
They said that they had all escaped from the sea
And asked very nicely if they could have tea
Mum asked them in and sat them all down
There was eight on the sofa and ten on the ground
There was three on an armchair and we thought there's no more
But there's one on a hook at the back of the door
"Har, har," said the Captain, "Har, har," said the Mate
"Har, har," said the cabin boy "Pass me a plate"
They started to nibble and gobble and grab
At the sandwiches filled up with fish-paste and crab
They sang of great treasures and songs of the sea
All the while they ate scones and drank gallons of tea
They all danced the hornpipe and amidst hoots and roars
They tapped out the rhythms on windows and doors
After an hour of this nautical fun
Where they munched all the sandwiches, tea-cakes and buns
The Captain said, "Mateys, let's give 'em three hips
Then it's time for us all to go back to our ships"
So off they departed, away from our street
Amidst shaking of hands and
tapping of feet
The neighbors came out and
shouted, "Hooray"
And hoped that the pirates
would come back one day
-Rob Erskine © (See Bio)

Oh what an imagination!

• • • • • • • • • • • • • • • • • •

Childhood, catching our imagination when it is fresh and tender, never lets go of us.

-J.B. Priestly

THE DRUM

I'm a beautiful red, red drum,
And I train with the soldier boys
As up the street we come,
Wonderful is our noise!
There's Tom, and Jim, and Phil,
And Dick, and Nat, and Fred,
While Widow Cutler's bill
And I march on ahead,
With a r-r-rat-tat-tat
And a tum-titty-um-tum-tum—
Oh, there's bushels of fun in that
For boys with a little red drum!

When I'm getting all dressed up, setting the table, caring for the babies, don't get the idea I'm "just playing". For, you see, I'm learning as I play; I may be a mother or a father someday.

Today, I am a child
and my work is play.
Won't you come to work with me?

Me, Myself and I

ME

As long as I live
I shall always be
My Self—and no other,
Just me.

Like a tree—
Willow, elder,
Aspen, thorn,
Or cypress forlorn.

Like a flower,
For its hour—
Primrose, or pink,
Or a violet—
Sunned by the sun,
And with dewdrops wet.

Always just me.
Till the day come on
When I leave this body,
It's all then done,
And the spirit within it
Is gone.
-Walter de la Mare

Yes, it's me
Wonderful
Loveable
Cuddly
Wiggly
Huggy
Happy
Messy
Noisy
Me!

240

Memories

PHOTOGRAPHS

Looking through the photographs,
Across the distant past;
Where did all the time go,
The years went by so fast.
Where is the little babe I held,
A bundle wrapped in blue;
I turned around and he was gone,
Is he somewhere, there in you?
When did you grow into a man,
Where is that little boy?
The one whose laughter filled the air,
As he raced from toy to toy.
Where is that silly, toothless grin,
And those precious tiny hands?
Are they still somewhere inside of you,
Now that you've become a man?
A Mother's heart will always see,
Across the distant past;
The babe she once held close in her arms,
In faded photographs.

-Allison Chambers Coxsey
©2000 (See Bio)

WHEN I WAS A BOY

Up in the attic where I slept
When I was a boy, a little boy,
In through the lattice the moonlight crept,
Bringing a tide of dreams that swept
Over the low, red trundle-bed,
Bathing the tangled curly head,
While moonbeams played at hide-and-seek
With the dimples on the sun-browned cheek---
When I was a boy, a little boy!
And, oh! the dreams—the dreams I dreamed!
When I was a boy, a little boy!
For the grace that through the lattice streamed
Over my folded eyelids seemed
To have the gift of prophecy,
And to bring me glimpses of times to be
When manhood's clarion seemed to call—
Ah! that was the sweetest dream of all,
When I was a boy, a little boy!
I'd like to sleep where I used to sleep
When I was a boy, a little boy!
For in at the lattice the moon would peep,
Bringing her tide of dreams to sweep
The crosses and griefs of the years away
From the heart that is weary and faint to-day;
And those dreams should give me back again
A peace I have never known since then—
When I was a boy, a little boy!

OVER THE HILLS AND FAR AWAY
A little boy steals from his morning play
And under the blossoming apple-tree
He lies and he dreams of the things to be:
Of battles fought and of victories won,
Of wrongs o'er thrown and of great deeds done
Of the valor that he shall prove some day,
Over the hills and far away
Over the hills, and far away!
Over the hills and far away
It's, oh, for the toil the livelong day!
But it mattereth not to the soul aflame
With a love for riches and power and fame!
On, O man! While the sun is high
On to the certain joys that lie
Yonder where blazeth the noon of day,
Over the hills and far away
Over the hills, and far away!
Over the hills and far away,
And old man lingers at close of day;
Now that his journey is almost done,
His battles bought and his victories won
The old-time honesty and truth,
The trustfulness and the friends of youth,
Home and mother—where are they?
Over the hills and far away
Over the years and far away!
-Eugene Field

MY FATHER

Who took me from my mother's arms
And, smiling at her soft alarms,
Showed me the world and nature's charms?
My Father.
Who made me feel and understand
The wonders of the sea and land,
And mark through all the Maker's hand?
My Father.
Who climbed with me the mountain height,
And watched my look of dread delight,
While rose the glorious orb of light?
My Father.
Who, from each flower and verdant stalk,
Gathered a honied store of talk
To fill the long, delightful walk?
My Father.
Not on an insect could he tread,
Nor strike the stinging nettle dead;
Who taught at once my heart and head?
My Father.
Who wrote upon that heart the line
Religion graved on Virtue's shrine,
To make the human race divine?
My Father.
Who taught my early mind to know
The god from whom all blessing flow,
Creator of all things below?
My Father
Who now, in pale and placid light
Of memory, gleams upon my sight,
Bursitn the sepulcher of night?
My Father.

My Mother

Who dressed my doll in clothes so gay,
And fondly taught me how to play,
And minded all I had to say?
My mother.
Who ran to help me when I fell,
And would some pretty story to tell,
Or kiss the place to make it well?
My mother.
Who taught my infant lips to pray,
And love God's holy book and day,
And walk in wisdom's pleasant way?
My Mother.
-Ann Taylor

How I wish the hands of time,
would slow down for a while.
So I could savor every moment
of nearness to my child.
For if I could, I'd stop the
clock and keep him here with me.
But when he's gone, I'll still hold on
to cherished memories.
(Excerpt from a poem by...)
Brenda Ball © 2001
Written for my wonderful son, Ethan

O, teach me still the Christian plan!
Thy practice with thy precept ran?
Nor yet desert me now a man,
My Father.
Still let thy pupil's heart rejoice
With charms of thy angelic voice,
Still prompt the motive and the choice,
My Father.
For yet remain a little space,
Till I shall meet thee face to face,
And not, as now, in vain embrace,
My Father.
Soon, and before the mercy-seat,
Spirits made perfect, we shall meet!
The with what transport shall I greet,
My Father.

The Days Gone By

O The days gone by! O the days gone by!
The apples in the orchard,
and the pathway through the rye;
The chirrup of the robin,
and the whistle of the quail
As he piped across the meadows
sweet as any nightingale;
When the bloom was on the clover,
and the blue was in the sky,
And my happy heart brimmed over,
in the days gone by.

MILESTONES

A TOUCH OF LOVE

You were six months old and full of fun
With a blink of my eye, you were suddenly one
There were so many things we were going to do,
But I turned my head and you turned two.
At two you were very dependant on me
But independence took over when you turned three.
Your third birthday, another year I tried to ignore,
But when I lit the candles, there weren't three, but four.
Four was the year that you really strived.
Why, look at you now, you're already five.
Now you are ready for books and for rules.
This is the year that you go to school.
The big day came, you were anxious to go.
We walked to the bus, going oh, so slowly.
As you climbed aboard and waved good-bye,
I felt a lump in my throat and tears stung my eyes.
Time goes so fast, it's hard to believe
That just yesterday you were home here with me.
And tomorrow, when the bus brings you home
and you jump to the ground,
You'll be wearing your cap and graduation gown.
So I'm holding to these moments as hard as I can,
Because the next time I look,
I'll be seeing a man.
-Unknown

My child, your memory treasures,
Captured in this book to see,
Creating it has been my pleasure,
This priceless gift to you
from me. -Kim Beckstead

Oh, the moments how they fly!

My one year old daughter
giggles with joy
And sparkles with glee,
she's sweetness and sunshine
as she looks at me.
One moment with her
And she'll steal your heart
What a blessing she's been
Right from the start.
Hugs and kisses
Dresses and bows
She's a miracle baby.
Every moment she grows.
-Linda LaTourelle

Miracles

EVERY CHILD IS A MIRACLE

It was a very special time, blessed by God above, When a new live was formed out of my dear parent's love. And every part of me was made with His infinite care...From inside out He fashioned me before they were aware. And soon my heart was beating, but still I was not whole, Until God breathed into me, and gave to me my soul. Created in His likeness, complete at last and free, God performed another miracle... When He created me!
-Dorothea Barwick © 1995

Lo, Children are a heritage of the LORD -Psalm 127:3

For I am fearfully and wonderfully made

☆ Miracles do happen

☆ You are a miracle to me

☆ Out of difficulties grow miracles

☆ I believe in miracles I believe in signs

☆ I believe that mountains move one prayer at a time

☆ Don't believe in miracles -- depend on them

Miscellaneous Topics

Freckles

- ◎ A face without freckles is like a night without stars
- ◎ Freckles are angel kisses
- ◎ Freckles are fairy's kisses
- ◎ Freckles are sun kisses

Happiness

- ◎ If you're happy and you know it clap your hands
- ◎ Laughter is the best medicine
- ◎ Belly laughs and tummy aches
- ◎ Miles of smiles
- ◎ We are a happy family
- ◎ Happy Days
- ◎ Big Grin
- ◎ A wink and a smile
- ◎ A giggle a day work play

Hats

- ◎ Caps for sale
- ◎ 'hat's all folks
- ◎ Love that hat
- ◎ So many hat's
- ◎ Kid in the hat
- ◎ Cat in the hat
- ◎ The mad hatter

☆ Miscellaneous

- ☆ A day to remember
- ☆ A lazy day
- ☆ Adventures in baby-sitting
- ☆ All by myself
- ☆ As time goes by
- ☆ Here's the scoop
- ☆ How time flies
- ☆ If I had a hammer...
- ☆ I'm goofy for you
- ☆ Me and my babysitter
- ☆ Monkeying around
- ☆ Mr/Miss Busybody
- ☆ Playroom Wars
- ☆ Playground Playmates
- ☆ Mom's/Dad's helper
- ☆ Memories of me
- ☆ Motor mouth
- ☆ Mr. Goodwrench
- ☆ Puttin on the ritz
- ☆ Simply Impish
- ☆ So blessed!
- ☆ Snow birds
- ☆ Snuggle bunny
- ☆ Snoopy do
- ☆ Special Memories
- ☆ Stay Tuned
- ☆ Too big for my britches
- ☆ Too tired to stop
- ☆ Totally Terrific
- ☆ They tremble at my sight
- ☆ The Big Bouncer
- ☆ The Great Day
- ☆ The star of the show
- ☆ The adventures of ____
- ☆ Mr. Doo Doo
- ☆ The Magnificent ____
- ☆ The way we look
- ☆ They call me ____
- ☆ Through the years
- ☆ Tool Time
- ☆ Tweet Success
- ☆ Udderly Unique
- ☆ We are blessed
- ☆ What a day!
- ☆ What a face!
- ☆ Winner of my heart

My Mother

Who fed me from her gently breast,
And hushed me in her arms to rest,
And on my cheek sweet kisses prest?
My Mother
When sleep forsook my open eye,
Who was it sang sweet lullaby,
And rocked me that I should not cry.
My mother
Who sat and watched my infant head,
When sleeping on my cradle bed,
And tears of sweet affection shed?
My Mother
When pain and sickness made me cry,
Who gazed upon my heavy eye,
And wept for fear that I should die?
My Mother
Who dressed my doll in clothes so gay,
And taught me pretty how to play,
And minded all I had to say?
My Mother
Who ran to help me when I fell,
And would some pretty story tell,
Or kiss the place to make it well?
My Mother
And can I ever cease to be
Affectionate and kind to thee,
Who was so very kind to me?
My Mother

Mother and Child

O Mother-My-Love, if you'll give me your hand,
And go where I ask you to wander,
I will lead you away to a beautiful land
The Dreamland that's waiting out yonder.
We'll walk in a sweet-posy garden out there
Where moonlight and starlight are streaming
And the flowers and the birds are filling the air
With the fragrance and music of dreaming.

There'll be no little tired-out boy to undress,
No questions or cares to perplex you;
There'll be no little bruises or bumps to caress,
Nor patching of stockings to vex you.
For I'll rock you away on a silver-dew stream,
And sing you asleep when you're weary,
And no one shall know of our beautiful dream
But you and your own little dearie.

And when I am tired I'll nestle my head
In the bosom that's soothed me so often,
And the wide-awake stars shall sing in my stead
A song which our dreaming shall soften.
-Eugene Field

Mother...
the sweetest name
a baby knows

A MOTHER'S SONG

Oh, come now, my darling,
And lie on my breast,
For that's the soft pillow
My baby loves best;
Peace rest on thine eyelids,
As sweetly they close,
And thoughts of tomorrow
Ne'er break thy repose.
What dreams in thy slumber,
Dear baby, are thine?
Thy sweet lips are smiling,
When pressed thus to mine.
All lovely and guileless
Thou sleepest in joy,
And heaven watches
over my beautiful boy.
Oh would thus that ever
My darling might smile,
And still be a baby
My griefs to beguile;
But hope whispers sweetly,
"Ne'er broken shall be
The tie that unites my
sweet baby to me."

MOTHERS AND DAUGHTERS

Why does it seem as I grow old,
The years speed on their way,
I seem more like my mother,
With all the things I say.
When I was young and on my own,
My mother seemed so square,
I rolled my eyes and told my self,
I'm never going there.
I am no longer in control,
Or so it seems to be,
I have become my mother's girl,
That's what they all tell me.
I have her mannerisms,
Her laughter and her voice,
No one thought to ask me,
I didn't have a choice.
I only wish that I had said,
While she was here to see,
If I can be just like you Mom,
That's what I want to be.
-Lorree O'Neil © (See Bio)

MOMMY'S SHOES

I like to wear my mommy's shoes.
I mean the pair she doesn't use.
I pick the ones with the highest heels,
You can't imagine how it feels.
To walk around, go out the door.
Clump-clumping all across the floor.
-Kate Gossard

MOTHER'S LOVE

A mother's soft and gentle touch,
Her caring, tender hands;
Know when her children need her,
They seem to understand.
They have a language of their own,
Communicate so well;
Speak softly to her children's hearts,
More than mere words can tell.
A mother's warm and loving arms,
Can soothe a baby's cry;
The sweetest song of tenderness,
In a mother's lullaby.
Her arms know when to hold them close,
And drive away their fears;
They comfort and protect you,
'til problems disappear.
A mother's kind, soft-spoken words,
Can be a soothing balm;
To smooth the stormy seas of life,
And make the waters calm.
Her soft voice whispers love to them,
Sings to them as they sleep;
Of angels that watch over them,
Of how they guard and keep.
There's nothing like! a mother's heart,
Her love...her prayers...her smile;
God placed these all within her,
To give back to her child.

• • • • • • • • • • • • • • • • • • •

THE MOTHER'S WISH

May cloudless beams of grace and truth
Adorn my daughter's opening youth;
Long, happy in her native home,
Among its fragrant groves to roam.
May choicest blessings her attend,
Blest in her parents, sisters, friend!
May no rude wish assail her breast
To love this world, by all confessed
As only given us to prepare
For one eternal, bright, and fair.
This world shall then no force retain,
Its siren voice shall charm in vain;
Religion's aid true peace shall bring,
Her voice with joy shall praises sing
To Him, whose streams of mercy flow
To cheer the heart o'er charg'd with wo;
And while retirement's sweets we prove,
For ever praise redeeming love.

♡

There's a dance
Between baby and mother
Soft and slow and sweet
On all earth there is no other
Than the dance between
baby and mother

NAUGHTY AND NICE

LITTLE MUDDY FEET

I waxed the floor just yesterday,
The house was clean and neat.
Out of nowhere tracks appeared from
"Little Muddy Feet".
I plopped down on the sofa,
Hands flew up in defeat.
Stomping in the mud again,
Those "muddy little feet".
Your shoes come off at eh door!?
I heard myself repeat.

NURSERY RHYMES

THREE LITTLE KITTENS

Three little kittens
Lost their Mittens;
And they began to cry,
"Oh! Mother dear,
We really fear
That we have lost
our mittens."
"Lost your mittens!
You naughty kittens!
Then you shall have no pie."
"Mee-ow, mee-ow, mee-ow."
"No, you shall have no pie."
Mee-ow, mee-ow, mee-ow.

Hey diddle-diddle,
The cat and the fiddle,
The cow jumped
over the moon;
The little dog laughed
to see such sport,
And the dish ran
away with the spoon.

Little Boy Blue, come blow your horn,
The sheep's in the meadow, the cow's in the corn.
Where's the little boy who looks after the sheep?
Under the haystack, fast asleep.
Will you wake him? No, not I,
For if I do, he's sure to cry.

Mary had a little lamb,
little lamb, little lamb.
Mary had a little lamb,
Its fleece was white as snow.

One for the money,
Two for the show,
Three to make ready,
And four to go!

1 2 3

Pat-a-cake, pat-a-cake, baker's man,
Bake me a cake as fast as you can.
Roll it, and prick it, and mark it with a "B"
And put it in the oven for Baby and me!

Mary Mary quite contrary,
How does your garden grow?
With silver bells and cockle shells
And pretty maids all in a row.

Jack and Jill went up the hill
to fetch a pail of water
Jack fell down and broke his crown
And Jill came tumbling after.

Little Jack Horner sat in the corner
Eating his Christmas pie,
He put in his thumb and pulled out a plum
And said "What a good boy am I!"

Diddle, diddle, dumpling, my son John,
Went to bed with his trousers on;
One shoe off, and one shoe on,
Diddle, diddle, dumpling, my son John!

This little piggy went to market,
This little piggy stayed home,
This little piggy had roast beef,
This little piggy had none,
And this little piggy cried,
Wee, wee, wee, all the way home.

One little, two little, three little Indians
Four little, five little, six little Indians
Seven little, eight little, nine little Indians
Ten little Indian boys.

There was an old woman who lived in a shoe.
She had so many children, she didn't know what to do.
She gave them some broth, without any bread,
Kissed them all sweetly, and sent them to bed.

Skip, skip, skip to my Lou,
Skip, skip, skip to my Lou,
Skip, skip, skip to my Lou,
Skip, to my Lou, my darlin'.

One I love, two I love,
Three I love, I say;
Four I love with all my heart,
Five I dance all day.

Old MacDonald had a farm, E-I-E-I-O.
And on his farm he had a cow, E-I-E-I-O.
With a moo, moo here and a moo, moo there,
Here a moo, there a moo,
Everywhere a moo-moo,
Old MacDonald had a farm, E-I-E-I-O.

Rain, rain, go away;
Come again another day;
Little _____ wants to play.

It's raining, it's pouring;
The old man is snoring.
Bumped his head
And he went to bed
And he couldn't get up in the morning

Mother May I?

London Bridge is falling down,
Falling down, falling down.
London Bridge is falling down,
My fair lady.

I scream,
You scream
We all scream
For ice cream!

This old man, he played one,
He played knick knack with his thumb,
With a Knick, knack, paddy whack,
Give the dog a bone;
This old man came rolling home

A tisket, A tasket,
A green and yellow basket,
I wrote a letter to my love,
And on the way, I dropped it.

Jack be nimble, Jack be quick,
Jack jump over the candle-stick

Handy Pandy, Jack-a-dandy,
Loves plum cake and sugar candy.
He bought some at a grocer's shop,
And out he came, hop, hop, hop!

Smiling girls, rosy boys,
Come and buy my little toys;
Monkeys made of gingerbread,
And sugar horses painted red.

One, two,
Buckle my shoe
Three, four
Knock at the door
Five, six,
Pick up sticks
Seven, eight
Lay them straight
Nine, ten
A big, fat hen

Little Tom Tucker
Little Tom Tucker
Sings for his supper.
What shall he eat?
White bread and butter.

John Jacob Jingleheimer Schmidt!
That's my name, too!
Whenever we go out,
The people always shout,
John Jacob Jingleheimer Schmidt!

Here we go round the mulberry bush,
The mulberry bush, the mulberry bush,
Here we go round the mulberry bush.
On a cold and frosty morning.

THE FARMER IN THE DELL

The farmer in the dell,
The farmer in the dell,
Hi-ho, the derry-o,
The farmer in the dell.
The farmer takes a wife,
The farmer takes a wife,
Hi-ho, the derry-o,
The farmer takes a wife.
The wife takes a child,
The wife takes a child,
Hi-ho, the derry-o,
The wife takes a child.

THE LITTLE GIRL THAT LIED

AND has my darling told a lie?
Did she forget that GOD was by?
That GOD, who saw the things she did,
From whom no action can be hid;
Did she forget that GOD could see
And hear, wherever she might be?
He made your eyes, and can discern
Whichever way you think to turn;
He made your ears, and he can hear
When you think nobody is near;
In every place, by night or day,
He watches all you do and say.

Boys and girls, come out to play.
The moon doth shine as bright as day!
Leaves your supper and leave your sleep,
And come with your playfellows into the street.
Come with a whistle,
Come with a call,
Come with a good will, or not at all.

♡

The ants go marching one by one.
Hurrah! Hurrah!
The ants go marching one by one.
Hurrah! Hurrah!
The ants go marching one by one;
The little one stops to suck his thumb,
And they all go marching
down
into the ground
to get out
of the rain.
Boom, boom, boom!

♡

Polly, put the kettle on,
Polly, put the kettle on,
Polly, put the kettle on,
We'll all have tea.

♡

Wash the dishes,
Wipe the dishes,
Ring the bell for tea;
Three good wishes,
Three good kisses,
I will give to thee.

Hickory Dickory Dock
Hickory Dickory Dock
The Mouse ran up the clock
The clock struck twelve
The mouse ran down
Hickory Dickory Dock

Winter
Cold and raw the north wind doth blow,
Bleak in the morning early;
All the hills are covered with snow,
And winter's now come fairly.

Fingers and Toes
Every lady in this land
Has twenty nails, upon each hand
Five, and twenty on hands and feet:
All this is true, without deceit.

Cross Patch
Cross patch, draw the latch,
Sit by the fire and spin;
Take a cup and drink it up,
Then call your neighbors in.

Tweedle-dum and Tweedle-dee
Tweedle-dum and tweedle-dee
Resolved to have a battle,
For tweedle-dum said tweedle-dee
Had spoiled his nice new rattle.

Pat-a-cake

Pat-a-cake, pat-a-cake,
Baker's man!
Bake me a cake
As fast as you can.
Pat it, and sift it
And throw it up high
Put it in the oven
For baby and I.

Little Jumping Joan

Here am I, little jumping Joan,
When nobody's with me
I'm always alone.

Robin Redbreast

Little robin redbreast sat upon a tree,
Up went pussy-cat, down went he,
Down came pussy-cat, away robin ran,
Says little robin redbreast: "catch me if you can!

Baby Dolly

Hush, baby, my dolly, I pray you don't cry,
And I'll give you some bread, and some milk by-and-by;
Or perhaps you like custard, or, maybe, a tart,
Then to either you're welcome, with all my heart.

I had a little hobby-horse and it was dapple gray

If Wishes Were Horses

If wishes were horses, beggars would ride.
If turnips were watches,
I would wear one by my side.
And if "ifs" and "ands"
Were pots and pans,
There'd be no work for tinkers!

To Market

To market, to market, to buy a fat pig,
Home again, home again, jiggety jig.
To market, to market, to buy a fat hog,
Home again, home again, jiggety jog.
To market, to market, to buy a plum bun,
Home again, home again, market is done.

Play Days

How many days has my baby to play?
Saturday, Sunday, Monday,
Tuesday, Wednesday, Thursday, Friday,
Saturday, Sunday, Monday.

Shoo Fly Shoo

Fly's in the buttermilk, shoo, shoo, shoo,
Fly's in the buttermilk, shoo, shoo, shoo,
Fly's in the buttermilk, shoo, shoo, shoo,
Skip, to my Lou, my darlin'.

Curly-Locks

Curly-locks, curly-locks, wilt thou be mine?
Thou shalt not wash the dishes,
nor yet feed the swine;
But sit on a cushion, and sew a fine seam,
And feed upon strawberries, sugar, and cream.

Humpty Dumpty

Humpty dumpty sat on a wall,
Humpty dumpty had a great fall;
All the king's horses, and all the king's men
Cannot put humpty dumpty together again.

Dance To Your Daddy

Dance to your daddy,
My bonnie laddie;
Dance to your daddy,
my bonnie lamb;
You shall get a fishy,
On a little dishy;
You shall get a fishy,
when the boat comes home.

Little Fred

When little Fred went to bed,
He always said his prayers;
He kissed mamma
and then papa,
And straightway
went upstairs.

The Alphabet Song
A B C D E F G
H I J K LMNOP
Q R S and T U V
W X and Y and Z.
Now I know my ABCs;
Next time won't you sing with me.

Happy Birthday to You
Happy birthday to you,
Happy birthday to you,
Happy birthday, dear friend,
Happy birthday to you

My Bonnie
My bonnie lies over the ocean.
My bonnie lies over the sea.
My bonnie lies over the ocean.
O bring back my bonnie to me.

Pease Porridge Hot
Pease porridge hot!
Pease porridge cold!
Pease porridge in the pot
Nine days old.

I Love You
I love you true
I love you blue
I love you
I do

• • • • • • • • • • • • • • • • • • •

Twinkle, Twinkle, Little Star

Twinkle, twinkle, little star,
How I wonder what you are!
Up above the world so high,
Like a diamond in the sky.
Twinkle, twinkle, little star,
How I wonder what you are!

When the blazing sun is gone,
When he nothing shines upon,
Then you show your little light,
Twinkle, twinkle, all the night.
Twinkle, twinkle, little star,
How I wonder what you are!

Then the traveler in the dark
Thanks you for your tiny spark;
He could not see which way to go,
If you did not twinkle so.
Twinkle, twinkle, little star,
How I wonder what you are!

In the dark blue sky you keep,
And often through my curtains peep,
For you never shut your eye
Till the sun is in the sky.
Twinkle, twinkle, little star,
How I wonder what you are!

This is the
original
poem/song
by Jane and
Anne Taylor
from c. 1806.

As your bright and tiny spark
Lights the traveler in the dark,
Through I know not what you are,
Twinkle, twinkle, little star.
Twinkle, twinkle, little star,
How I wonder what you are!

271

Baa, Baa, Black Sheep

Baa, baa, black sheep,
Have you any wool?
Yes sir, yes sir,
Three bags full;
One for my master,
One for my dame,
But none for the little boy
Who cries in the lane.

Hobby Horse

I had a little hobby-horse,
and it was dapple gray;
Its head was made of pea-straw,
its tail was made of
hay,

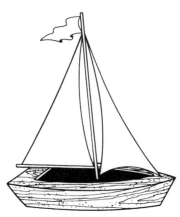

I Saw A Ship A-Sailing

I saw a ship a-sailing,
A-sailing on the sea;
And, oh! It was all laden
With pretty, things for thee!

272

One, He Loves

One, he loves; two, he loves:
Three, he loves, they say;
Four, he loves with all his heart;
Five, he casts away.
Six, he loves; seven, she loves;
Eight, they both love.
Nine, he comes; ten, he tarries;
Eleven, he courts; twelve, he marries

For Baby

You shall have an apple,
You shall have a plum,
You shall have a rattle,
When papa comes home.

The Queen of Tarts

The queen of hearts,
She made some tarts,
All on a summer's day;
The knave of hearts,
He stole the tarts,
And took them clean away.

Georgie Porgie

Georgie Porgie, pudding and pie,
Kisses the girls and made them cry;
When the girls begin to play,
Georgie Porgie runs away.

Park and Playground

I PREFER THE SLIDE

Some people say they love to swing
While others like to ride
The horses on the merry-go-round
And others love the slide.
When I go to the park
The most fun I have found
Is climbing to the slide's tip top
And then zooming to the ground.
So happily I slide along
And too quickly do I land
On my feet or on my bottom
In the nice warm sand!
I do not hesitate at all!
But slides like every other game
Are more fun with a friend !
-Thena Smith ©

Play is often talked about as if it were a relief from serious learning. But for children play is serious learning. Play is really the work of childhood. -Fred Rogers

PLAYGROUND FUN

Oh how I love to swing in the swing
And go up in the air so high!
I think that someday when I swing
My feet might touch the sky!
I love to slide down the slide
And land on the soft brown sand.
I like go zooming down the slide
And I like it when I land!
I like to sit on the grass and play
And find a bug or two.
I love to go to the playground
'Cause there's so much for kid to do!
-Thena Smith ©

THREE KINDS OF SEE-SAW

See-saw I saw
In the fields one day;
A see-saw you'll see
When the children play;-
And oh! the very
Funniest way
To see a see-saw,
I know you'll say,
Is when at the biggest
Show in town,
The elephants see-saw,
Up and down!
-Mary Mapes Dodge

Park

☆ Play day, play day, everyday is my way

☆ Play today, sleep tomorrow

☆ Playing Dirty playing in the mud

☆ Playing Dress up

☆ Playing With My Toys

☆ I'd rather be playing

☆ Sleep...No Play

☆ A child reminds us that playtime is an essential part of our daily routine

☆ There's nothing like playing dress up with your best friend

☆ Playtime, it's my favorite time

☆ All play and no work is cool

☆ Playmate come out and play with me

☆ Play Day at the Park

☆ I LOVE to Play

☆ Getting' down and dirty

☆ Sand in my eyes, sand in my hair, my oh, my sand everywhere

☆ Dirt cakes and mud muffins keep a boy fed

- A hard day's play
- Barefoot in the park
- Climin' Time
- Games Kids Play
- Havin' a all
- In the swing of things
- Inside, outside, upside down
- Jumpin, for joy
- Just hangin' out together
- Just swingin' so high
- Kids at play
- Kids' choice award
- Me and my toys
- Mom's Day at the Park
- Outside
- Play Date
- Play is hard work
- Playing around the playground
- Pretending is fun
- Saturday in the Park
- See ay Play!
- See-Saw, Up we go
- Swingin' around
- Take the time to play
- Up, Up, and Away
- Warning! Children at play!
- Wild and crazy kids

277

Party

FIRST ARRIVALS

'It is a party, do you know,
And there they sit, all in a row,
Wait till the others come,
To begin to have some fun.
Wonder what they'll have for tea;
Hope the jam is strawberry.
Wonder what the dance and game;
Feel so very glad they came.
Very Happy may you be,
May you much enjoy your tea.

- Birthday Bash
- Birthday Bonanza
- For me?
- Celebrate!
- I wish for...
- It's My Birthday
- It's my party and I'll cry if I want to!
- Just what I've always wanted
- Let's Party
- Make a Wish
- M'mm! Good

- Time for Cake
- Today Is Your Day
- Under Wraps
- We need more candles
- Where's the Party
- You can't have your cake and eat it to
- You can't wear your cake and eat it too
- Super Baby Party
- Party til you poop
- Party Babe
- Having Fun Now

- _____ Is One-Derful!
- And A Pinch To Grow An Inch
- Bearly One Year Old
- Big Boy/Girl
- Birthday Bash
- Birthday Bonanza
- Birthday Girl/Boy
- Birthday Party Number One - I Am Having So Much Fun!
- Born To Party
- Choo-Choo! _____ Turns Two
- Fantastic Fours
- Forever Young
- Fun Being One
- Happy Birthday To You
- Have A Dino-Mite Birthday
- I Wish For...
- It's Fun To Be One
- It's My Birthday
- It's My Party And I'll Cry If I Want To!
- It's Party Time!
- Let Me Eat Cake
- Let Them Eat Cake
- Let's Celebrate _____
- Let's Party
- Look At Me . . . I Am Three!
- Look How Big I'm Getting
- Make A Wish
- Mmm...Good!
- Now I Am ___, I'm Clever As Clever
- One Is Wonderful
- One Year Older And Cuter, Too
- Parties Are Wonderful!
- Party Girl/Boy

- Present Time
- Ready, Set, Blow
- So Many Candles...So Little Cake
- So Many Presents, So Little Time!
- Star Of The Party
- Surprise!
- Terrific Two's
- That Takes The Cake
- The Big One
- The More Candle The Bigger The Wish
- The Party's Here
- There's No Time Like The Presents!
- They Grow Up So Fast
- Thrilling Three's
- Time For Cake
- Today Is Your Day
- Under Wraps

- We Need More Candles
- We're Havin' Some Fun Now
- Where's The Party?
- You Can Have Your Cake And Eat It Too
- You Can Wear Your Cake And Eat It Too
- You Take The Cake
- You're Getting Better

Just twelve short months ago I made my big debut so now I'd like to celebrate My first birthday with you

280

• • • • • • • • • • • • • • • • • • •

PETS AND ANIMALS
PUPPY LOVE

I was driving down the highway,
In the middle of nowhere,
I passed a little ball of fur,
Who turned her head to stare,
With that my heart turned over,
I could not leave her there,
Frightened, lost and shivering,
Cause someone didn't care.
I took her home and bathed her,
She was such a sorry sight,
But I shuddered as I thought about,
What might have been her plight.
I didn't need a puppy,
But what else could I have done,
And I hated to admit it,
But, doggone it, she was fun.
She took over my house,
Right from the very start,
As she wiggled and she squirmed,
Her way into my heart.
Her needs now all came first,
Her wish was my command,
My reward was a gently kiss,
A wet nose in my hand.
She soon became my shadow,
Went everywhere with me,
No longer was I lonely,
Though I had no privacy.
I instead, I had undying trust
Like I had never know,
Just for picking up this waif,
And giving her a home.
-Loree O'Neil © 2003 (See Bio)

- 2 bossy dogs live here
- A bone to pick
- A boy and his dog
- A dog is a man's best friend
- A dog says "I love you" with his tail
- A dog's life
- A spoiled, rotten poodle lives with me
- Agenda for the day: let the dog in, let the dog out
- A little cat nap
- Alley cat
- Cats don't have owners...they have staff
- Cat's in the cradle
- Cats/Dogs are just children with fur!
- Curious kitty
- Fat cat
- Fur-Rocious fun
- Purrfect
- The cats meow
- The cat's pajamas
- Meow spoken here
- My cat is my best friend
- Love me, Love my cat
- When the cat's away, the mice will play
- When you have a cat every day is purrfect
- Will work for tuna
- Sittin' pretty with my kitty
- The cat in the hat
- Just cat-napping
- Kitten Kaboodle
- Kitten on the keys
- Love that cat
- Meow

- "Barnyard Animals"
- "cow"nt your blessings
- A horse with no name
- A whale of a good time
- A whale of a time
- Barnyard buddies
- Cowabunga!!!
- Ewe are loved
- Farm fresh
- Going whole hog
- Hog wild
- Hogs and kisses
- Horse sense
- I love ewe
- Just horsin' around
- Moo time
- My little pony
- Pony tale
- The mane event
- This little piggy

MY PUPPY
Here sits my puppy
All tattered and torn
Everybody loves him
Even thought he's so worn
His body is a mess
But I love him dearly
And he loves me best!

CATS AND DOGS
Dad says it's raining cats and dogs,
I said, You're off your noodle.
Until I went outside to see
And stepped into a poodle!
-Rod Erskine © (See Bio)

PICNIC

Picnic in the Park

Oh what fun to picnic in the park!
Oh what a wonderful way
To enjoy the sun and have some fun
And spend a lovely day!

Oh what fun to sit in the grass
And drink lemonade in the shade!
What fun to eat from a picnic basket
Things so lovingly made!

But the the most special thing
That ever I could do
Is to go on a picnic
In the park with You!
-Thena ©

AT PLAY

Play that you are mother dear,
And play that papa is your beau;
Play that we sit in the corner here,
Just as we used to, long ago.
Playing so, we lovers two
Are just as happy as we can be
And I'll say "I love you" to you,
And you say "I love you" to me!
"I love you" we both shall say,
All in earnest and all in play.

MAKING MUD-PIES

Under the apple tree, spreading and thick,
Happy with only a pan and a stick,
On the soft grass in the shadow that lies,
Our little Fanny is making mud-pies.
On her brown apron and bright drooping head
Showers of pink and white blossoms are shed;
Tied to a branch that seems meant just for that,
Dances and flutters her little straw hat.

Children will soon forget
your presents. They will always
remember your presence.

THE BOX OF SAND

Just back of the house, right under a tree,
Is a box that is full of silver sand—
Of sand that was washed by a saltless sea
Till it rivals the white of a woman's hand;
And out of that box of sand arise
Such wonderful sights as never before
Were spoken of lips or seen of eyes.
And all the within sight of our back door.
There's an old pie-tin, with numberless holes,
A shovel, a rake and an old tin can,
A block of wood, and oh, dear souls!
In the midst of these is a working man;
He is busily making pies and cakes
And digging and sifting and playing store,
The which a hole in his stomach makes,
Which he brings to fill at our back door.

Girls and boys, come out to play,
the moon doth shine as bright as day,
Leave your supper and leave your sleep,
And come with your playfellows into the street.
Come with a whoop or come with a call,
Come with a goodwill or not at all.
Up the ladder and down the wall,
A halfpenny roll will serve us all.
You find milk and I'll find flour,
And we'll have a pudding in half an hour!

Take time to play
Just for today
Memories will come
Just have some fun

So many toys, so little time

Playmate come out
and play with me

Housework can wait, my children need kisses
They want me to play, I'll put off the dishes
When they're grown,
I'll keep the house spic and span...
But children grow fast so I'll play while I can.

BLOCK CITY

What are you able to build with your blocks?
Castles and palaces, temples and docks.
Rain may keep raining, and others go roam,
But I can be happy and building at home.

Let the sofa be mountains, the carpet be sea,
There I'll establish a city for me:
A kirk and a mill and a palace beside,
And a harbor as well where my vessels may ride.

Great is the palace with pillar and wall,
A sort of a tower on the top of it all,
And steps coming down in an orderly way
To where my toy vessels lie safe in the bay.

This one is sailing and that one is moored:
Hark to the song of the sailors on board!
And see on the steps of my palace, the kings
Coming and going with presents and things!

Now I have done with it, down let it go!
All in a moment the town is laid low.
Block upon block lying scattered and free,
What is there left of my town by the sea?

Yet as I saw it, I see it again,
The king and the palace, the ships and the men,
And as long as I live, and where'er I may be,
I'll always remember my town by the sea.
-Robert Louis Stevenson

SHUFFLE-SHOON AND AMBER-LOCKS

Shuffle-Shoon and Amber-Locks
Sit together, building blocks;
Shuffle-Shoon is old and gray,
Amber-Locks a little child,
But together at their play
Age and Youth are reconciled,
And with sympathetic glee
Build their castles fair to see.
"When I grow to be a man"
(So the wee one's prattle ran),
"I shall build a castle so—
With a gateway broad and grand;
Here a pretty vine shall grow,
There a soldier guard shall stand;
And the tower shall be so high,
Folks will wonder, by and by!"
Shuffle-Shoon quoth: "Yes, I know;
Thus I builded long ago!
Here a gate and there a wall,
Here a window, there a door;
Here a steeple wondrous tall
Riseth ever more and more!
But the years have leveled low
What I builded long ago!"
So they gossip at their play,
Heedless of the fleeting day;
One speaks of the Long Ago
Where his dead hopes buried lie;
One with chubby cheeks aglow
Prattleth of the By and by;
Side by side, they build their blocks—
Shuffle-Shoon and Amber-Locks.
-Eugene Fields

• • • • • • • • • • • • • •

I had a little tea party
One afternoon at three
T'was very small
Just I, myself, and me.
Myself ate up the sandwiches
While I drank up the tea
T'was also I who ate the pie
And passed the cake to me.

A house
of cards
is neat
and small;
Shake
the
table,
Shake
the
table!
Watch them
fall !
Now that's

fun!

☺ A Doll's House
☺ A Little Never Hurt
☺ Be Happy Each Day
☺ Be Merry And Smile
☺ Build Sandcastles
☺ Dress Up The Cat
☺ Games Kids Play
☺ Get A Kite To Fly
☺ Go Barefootin'
☺ Havin' A Ball
☺ Hold Mom's Hand
☺ Jump In The Puddles
☺ Jumpin For Joy

☺ Kids Choice Award
☺ Make Mud Pies
☺ Me And My Toys
☺ Play In The Sand
☺ See...See...Play!
☺ Climbin' up so high
☺ Swing Time!
☺ Swing Up So High
☺ Swingin' Around
☺ Take Time To Play
☺ Toy Land
☺ Toy Story
☺ ____'S Playhouse!

PLAYMATES

If friendship were a color
You would be a rainbow to me!

THE UNSEEN PLAYMATE

When children are playing alone on the green,
In comes the playmate that never was seen.
When children are happy and lonely and good,
the friend of the children comes out of the wood.
Nobody heard him and nobody say,
His is a picture you never could draw,
But he's sure to be present, abroad or at home,
When children are happy and playing alone.
He lies in the laurels, he runs on the grass,
He sings when you tinkle the musical glass;
Whene'er you are happy and cannot tell why
The Friend of the Children is sure to be by!
He loves to be little, he hates to be big,
'T is he that inhabits the caves that you dig;
'T is he when you play with your soldiers of tin
That sides with the Frenchmen and never can win.
'T is he, when at night you go off to your bed,
Bids you go to your sleep and not trouble your head;
For wherever they're lying, in cupboard or shelf,
'T is he will take care of your playthings himself!
-Robert Louis Stevenson

There's nothing like a friend
to play with all day!

Pony (Knee) Rides

THE RIDER OF THE KNEE

Knightly Rider of the Knee
Of Proud-prancing Uncle!
Gaily mount, and wave the sign
Of that master of thine.

Pat thy steed and turn him free,
Knightly Rider of the Knee!
Sit thy charger as a throne
Lash him with thy laugh alone:

Sting him only with the spur
Of such with as may occur,
Knightly Rider of the Knee,
In they shriek of ecstasy.

Would, as now, we might endure,
Twain as one—thou miniature
Ruler, at the rein of me
Knightly Rider of the Knee!

Giddy up horsey,
giddy up and go

Ride a horse to Banbury Cross

I Love Ponies
I Love You
Whoa!

THE RIDE TO BUMPVILLE

Play that my knee was a calico mare
Saddled and bridled for Bumpville;
Leap to the back of this steed, if you dare,
And gallop away to Bumpville!
I hope you'll be sure to sit fast in your seat,
For this calico mare is prodigiously fleet,
And many adventures you're likely to meet
As you journey along to Bumpville.
This calico mare both gallops and trots
While whisking you off to Bumpville'
She paces, she shies, and she stumbles, in spots,
In the tortuous road to Bumpville;
And sometimes this strangely mercurial steed
Will suddenly stop and refuse to proceed,
Which, all will admit, is vexatious indeed,
When one is en rout to Bumpville!
She's scared of the cars when the engine goes "Toot!"
Down by the crossing at Bumpville;
You'd better look out for that treacherous brute
Bearing you off to Bumpville!
With a snort she rears up on her hindermost heels,
And executes jigs and Virginia reels—
Words fail to explain how embarrassed one feels
Dancing so wildly to Bumpville!
It's bumpytybump and it's jiggtyjog,
Journeying on to Bumpville;
It's over the hilltop and down through the bog
You ride on your way to Bumpville;
Ti's rattleybang over boulder and stump,
There are rivers to ford, there are fences to jump,
And the corduroy road it goes bumpytybump,
Mile after mile to Bumpville!
-Eugene Field

Potty Training

First you bought me diapers
Then you take them away
And give me what you call
training pants that's really
strange, I'd say!
Now you set this silly potty
Right in front of me
And tell me that
s where I am to sit
If I should have to "pee".
Well, I think this
is all really silly
But I want to do
what I should do
So I sit here on
this potty
-Thena Smith ©

It's my potty and I'll go if I want to...

- Grin and Swish it
- It's a Party in the Potty!!
- It's my potty and I'll cry if I want to!
- My kids love to potty all the time
- Naughty in the Potty
- You bowl me over
- Potty Animals
- We fought the Potty and the Potty won!
- A whole lot of pottying goin' on
- Caught in the Pot
- Fell in...Help!
- Potty Party
- Put on your big girl panties and deal with it

BIG KID NOW

I used to wear a diaper
When I was very little
They were held on with little tabs
And gave me a bulging middle!
I didn't know any better then
And wet them all day through
Until my mommy brought me a little potty chair
And said, "This is for you!"
It took a while to like this chair
And to sit there when I had to go
But one day I learned some things
That all the big kids know!
If I sit on my special chair
And do what's meant to be
It makes life much more fun
For mommy and for me!
I don't have to have saggy pads
Hanging to my knees
And it makes me more comfy
And my mommy it seems to please.
Yesterday, she brought me something else
I thought that I would share—
I haven't had this stuff before
She called it underwear!
-Thena Smith ©

I'm a big kid now!
Look mom, no diaper!

• • • • • • • • • • • • • • • • • •

PRAYERS

A CHILD PRAYING

Fold thy little hands in prayer,
Boy down at thy mother's knee,
Now thy sunny face is fair,
Shining through thine auburn hair;
Thine eyes are passion-free;
And pleasant thoughts, like garlands, bind thee
Unto thy home, yet grief may find thee—
Then pray, child, pray!
Now thy young heart, like a bird,
Warbles in its summer nest;
No evil thought, no unkind world,
No chilling autumn winds have stirred
The beauty of thy rest;
But winter hastens, and decay
Shall waste thy verdant home away—
Then pray, child, pray!
Thy bosom is a house of glee,
With gladness harping at the door;
While ever, with a joyous shout,
Hope, the May queen, dances out,
Her lips with music running o'er;
But Time those strings of joy will sever,
And hope will not dance on for ever—
Then pray, child, pray!
Now, thy mother's arm is spread
Beneath thy pillow in the night;
And loving feet creep round thy bed,
And o'er thy quiet face is shed
The taper's darkened light;
But that fond arm will pass away,
By thee no more those feet will stay—
Then pray, child, pray!
-Robert Aris Willmott

295

• • • • • • • • • • • • • • • • • •

A CHILD'S PRAYER

God, make my life a little light
Within the world to glow;
A little flame that burneth bright
Wherever I may go.
God, make my life a little flower
That giveth joy to all,
Content to bloom in native bower,
Although the place be small.
God, make my life a little song
That comforteth the sad,
That helpeth others to be strong
And makes the singer glad.
God, make my life a little staff
Whereon the weak may rest,
And so what health and strength I have
May serve my neighbors best.
God, make my life a little hymn
Of tenderness and praise;
Of faith, that never waxeth dim,
In all His wondrous ways.
-M. Betham-Edwards

GOD Bless thee, little lady,
Is my prayer on bended knee—
GOD guard and guide the precious child
Who is all the world to me.

These little hands are held in prayer,
To thank you, God for being there.
These little hearts speak to You,
To ask you, God what we should do.
These little eyes are filled with love,
For God in heaven up above.
Amen.

Thank You, God, for this new day,
And for the time to work and play,
Please be with me all day long,
In every story, game, and song.
May all the happy things we do
Make You, our Father, happy too.
Amen.

Now before I run to play,
Let me not forget to pray
To God who kept me
through the night
And waked me with the
morning light.
Help me, Lord to love Thee more
Than I ever loved before,
In my work and in my play,
Be Thou with me through the day.
Amen.

Dear Lord,
Please hear my prayer
Keep me in your ever care
Guide my dreams all through the night
Wake me with sweet morning light
Amen.

All things bright and beautiful,
All creatures great and small,
All things wise and wonderful,
The Lord God made them all.

Thank You for the world so sweet;
Thank You for the food we eat;
Thank You for the birds that sing;
Thank You, God, for everything!
Amen.
-E. Rutter Leatham

Keep our baby safe and strong,
Let his time with us be long,
Help us teach him right from wrong,
And we shall praise thee all day long.

How I love you, oh so much
God protect you with his touch.

A Prayer for My Child
Little Baby on the way
Getting bigger every day,
Kicking Mommy everywhere,
You are truly an answered prayer.

A PRAYER IN SPRING

Oh, give us pleasure in the flowers today;
And give us not to think so far away
As the uncertain harvest'keep us here
All simply in the springing of the year
Oh, give us pleasure in the orchard white,
Like nothing else by day, like ghosts by night:
And make us happy in the happy bees,
The swarm dilating round the perfect trees.
And make us happy in the darting bird
That suddenly above the bees is heard,
The meteor that thrusts in with needle bill,
And off a blossom in mid air stands still.
For this is love and nothing else is love,
That which it is reserved for God above
To sanctify to what far ends He will,
But which it only needs that we fulfill.
-Robert Frost

Please help us Lord, we pray to Thee
With thankful heart, on bended knee,
To raise this child that he might be,
A happy child because of me.
-Tina Greenfield

Around the throne of God in heaven
Thousands of children shout—
Children whose sins are all forgiven,
A holy, happy band
Singing, Glory, glory

DEAR FATHER, HEAR AND BLESS

Dear Father,
Hear and bless
Thy beasts
And singing birds:
And guard
With tenderness
Small things that have no words.

GRACE FOR A CHILD

Here a little child I stand,
Heaving up my either hand;
Cold as paddocks though they be,
Here I lift them up to Thee,
For a benison to fall
On our meat and on us all.
Amen
--Robert Herrick

DAY BY DAY

Day by day, dear Lord, of Thee
Three things I pray:
To see Thee more clearly,
Love Thee more dearly,
Follow Thee more nearly,
Day by day.

Morning Prayer

Now, before I run to play
Let me not forget to pray
To go who kept me throughout the night
And waked me with the morning light

Be present at our table, Lord,
Be here and everywhere adored.
These morsels bless, and grant that we
May feast in Paradise with Thee. Amen.

Evening Prayer

Now I lay me down to sleep,
I pray Thee, Lord, Thy child to keep:
Thy love guard me through the night,
And wake me with the morning light.

Good Night Prayer

Father, unto thee I pray,
Thou has guarded me all day;
Safe I am while in thy sight,
Safely let me sleep tonight.
Bless my friends, the whole world bless;
Help me to learn helpfulness;
Keep me ever in Thy sight;
So to all I say good night.

-Henry Johnstone

Pregnancy

- In Full Bloom...
- Mommy to Be
- Kid Under Construction
- I'm Pregnant...This is as Perky as I Get!
- It Started With a Kiss...And Ended Like This
- Super Uncomfortable...Thanks!
- Twinkle, Twinkle, Our Little Star
  How we Wonder What You Are
- Watch Me Grow

Waiting for You

Waiting for you
With hearts full of love
Our bundle of joy
From Heaven above.
Waiting to hold you
And look in your face
To give you my kisses
And a gentle embrace.
Mommy and Daddy
How happy we'll be
When you join our family
And we become Three!
-Thena Smith ©

• • • • • • • • • • • • • • • • •

PRESCHOOL & SCHOOL

THE FIRST DAY OF SCHOOL

New clothes in the closet, New shoes by the bed
He gets kind of worried as thoughts fill his head
The first day of school the times come at last
Will he like his new teacher? Who will be in his class?
Mother makes breakfast as she has always done
And tries to assure him that he will have fun
The world never seemed like such a big place
Now dressed and ready, his heart starts to race
At his new classroom his mother gives him a hug
When a child grabs his shirt and gives it a tug
Please come over and play with me
They have toys, games, and books come and see
His mother slips out and goes back home
She looks out the window and back at the phone
Wondering and hoping her boy is all right
Finally the school bus pulls into sight
She walks out to meet him so the bus finds their place
The doors swing open, there's a smile on his face
She chokes back a tear as she takes his hand
Her little boy has become her little man...
-Barbara K. Cox

Oh that first day of school is tough for mom
But fun for her baby
ABC 123 XYZ
How did my baby
get so big?

Our Little Princess

You are our Cinderella
Our little princess of a girl
You may not wear a slipper of glass
But you give our hearts a whirl.
We watch you with your storybook princess
And see your eyes aglow
But we feel that way
when we look at you
And just want you to know.
You make our home a castle
And our life is better than
Any fairy tale could ever be
For you are a real life little princess
So precious to your daddy and me!

♡ I'm a Princess! That's why!

♡ I'm a Princess, a Princess in training.

♡ I'm a Princess but I am in training to be a Queen

♡ It's not easy being a princess.

♡ It's not easy being a princess, but someone has got to do it!

♡ Princess of today, Queen of tomorrow!

♡ What part of Princess....don't you understand?

♡ Prince/Princess of my heart

LITTLE PRINCESS

Little princess that runs through the meadow
Dressed up in her prettiest gown
Looking for someone to play with
But no one is ever around
She dances through fields fresh with flowers
Their fragrance hangs thick in the air
Her voice hums a tune as she frolics
Oblivious to the world's every care!
Fairy sprites watched from a distance
They'd seen the small princess before
Afraid to let on that they lived there
They never lingered for long
Too scared were the fairies of humans
So frightened they hid in the grass
And ran when the princess came closer
Too late they heard her small gasp
At first she thought she was dreaming
She blinked and her eyes grew quite round
Her moth formed an O as she listened
To the fairy sprites running around
Her small hands reached out to touch them
And her voice was as soft as the breeze
Somehow they knew they could trust her
As they hid in the bushes and trees
They spent the whole day playing leap frog
They sang and they danced all around
The day ended over so quickly
The sun was soon going down
A happy day spent in the meadow
She knew she would come back tomorrow
To play with the friends she had met.

-Sandra Prouse © (See Bio)

Princess of Everything!

With a pretty dress
And lovely bow in my hair
I like to dress like a princess
When I go anywhere.
My lovely room is my castle
And my parents are queen and king.
With my dolly always at my side,
I'm princess of everything!
I'd love to be like Cinderella
And go to the ball some night
Or visit with those little folks
Like the beautiful Snow White.
A princess has a lovely life
And her job is to be sweet
Acting in a princess like way
To every one she meets!
I treat my dolly kindly
And never fuss or scold her
She is content to have
A princess mom to hold her.
-Thena Smith ©

♡ Cuz I'm the Princess/
   Prince, that's why!

♡ Damsel in Distress

♡ Pretty, pretty princess

♡ Princess Petunia

♡ Fussy Little Princess/Prince

PROVERBS

It's hard to train a child
In the way he should go,
If you don't go
That way yourself.

♡ A child's greatest period of growth is the month after you've bought new school clothes.

♡ A rich child often sits in a poor mother's lap.

♡ Anyone who says "...easy as taking candy from a baby", has never tried it.

♡ Children will soon forget your presents; they will always remember your presence.

♡ Don't give up, Moses was a basket case, too.

♡ Patience is the mother of a beautiful child.

♡ The best inheritance parents can give their children is a few minutes of their time each day.

♡ The jewel of the air is the sun; the jewel of the house is the child.

♡ There is only one pretty child in the world.. And every mother has it. -Chinese proverb

♡ To understand your parent's love you must raise children yourself.

♡ Who are these kids and why are they calling me MOM?

♡ Who takes the child by the hand, takes the mother by the heart.

AS I WAS GOING UP THE STAIR

As I was going up the stair
I met a man who wasn't there.
He wasn't there again today—
Oh, how I wish he'd go away

Ladybird! Ladybird!

Ladybird! Ladybird!
fly away home;
The field mouse is
gone to her nest,
The daisies have shut
up their sleepy red eyes,
And the birds and the
bees are at rest.
Ladybird! Ladybird!
fly away home;
The glowworm is
lighting her lamp,
The dew's falling
fast, and her fine
speckled wings
Will flag with the
close-clinging damp.
Ladybird! Ladybird!
fly away home;
To your house in the old hollow tree,
Where your children so dear have invited the ant
And a few cozy neighbors to tea.

BUG IN A JUG

Curious fly,
Vinegar jug,
Slippery edge,
Pickled bug.
-Anonymous

LITTLE BO PEEP

Little Bo Peep,
has lost her sheep,
And can't tell
where to find them;
Leave them alone,
and they'll come home.
Wagging their tails
behind them.

I will make you Toys for your delight
Of birdsong at morning and star shine at night.
I will make a palace fit for you and me,
Of green days in forests and blue days at sea.
-Robert Louis Stevenson

HIGGLEDY, PIGGLEDY MY BLACK HEN

Higgledy, Piggledy.
My black hen.
She lays eggs for gentlemen;
Sometimes nine, and sometimes ten.
Higgledy, Piggledy,
My black hen!

• • • • • • • • • • • • • • • •

Scripture

♡ As a father has compassion on his children, so the Lord has compassion on those who fear him *Ps. 103:13*

♡ Children's children are a crown to the aged, and parents are the pride of their children *Prov. 17:6*

♡ He settles the barren woman in her home as a happy mother of children. Praise the Lord! *Psalms 113:9*

♡ Yet you brought me out of the womb; you made me trust in you even at my mother's breast *Psalms 22:9*

♡ From birth I have relied on you; you brought me forth from my mother's womb. I will ever praise you *Psalms 71:6*

♡ For you created my inmost being; you knit me together in my mother's womb *Psalms 139:13*

♡ May your father and mother be glad; may she who gave you birth rejoice! *Proverbs 23:25*

♡ As a mother comforts her child, so will I comfort you; and you will be comforted over Jerusalem *Isaiah 66:1*

♡ Honor your father and mother... *Deuteronomy 5:16*

♡ And thou shalt teach them diligently unto thy children, and shalt talk of them when thou sittest in thine house, and when thou walkest by the way, and when thou liest down, and when thou risest up *Deuteronomy 6:7*

You are a child of the King

SEASONS
BED IN SUMMER

In winter I get up at night
And dress by yellow candle-light.
In summer, quite the other way,
I have to go to bed by day.
I have to go to bed and see
The birds still hopping on the tree,
Or hear the grown-up people's feet
Still going past me in the street.
And does it not seem hard to you,
When all the sky is clear and blue,
And I should like so much to play,
To have to go to bed by day?

-Robert Louis Stevenson

A PRAYER IN SPRING

Oh, give us pleasure in the flowers today;
And give us not to think so far away
As the uncertain harvest' keep us here
All simply in the springing of the year.
Oh, give us pleasure in the orchard white,
Like nothing else by day, like ghosts by night:
And make us happy in the happy bees,
The swarm dilating round the perfect trees.
And make us happy in the darting bird
That suddenly above the bees is heard,
The meteor that thrusts in with needle bill,
And off a blossom in mid air stands still.
For this is love and nothing else is love,
The which it is reserved for God above
To sanctify to what far ends He will,
But which it only needs that we fulfill.

-Robert Frost

311

Come said the wind to the leaves one day,
Come o're the meadows and we will play.
Put on your dresses scarlet and gold,
For summer is gone and the days grow cold."
-A Children's Song of the 1880's

"No spring nor summer beauty hath such grace
as I have seen in one autumnal face"
-John Donne

"Have patience. All things change in due time.
Wishing cannot bring autumn glory
or cause winter to cease."
-Ginaly-li, Cherokee

"The October day is a dream,
bright and beautiful as the rainbow,
and as brief and fugitive."
-W. Hamilton Gibson

"In heaven it is always autumn,
His mercies are ever in their maturity."
-John Donne

"...The winds will blow their own freshness into you,
and the storms their energy,
while cares will drop away from you
like the leaves of Autumn."
-John Muir

"Delicious autumn! My very soul is wedded to it,
and if I were a bird I would fly about the earth
seeking the successive autumns."
-George Eliot

"

I thought that spring must last forevermore for I was young and loved, and it was May -Vera Brittain

If we had no winter, the spring would not be so pleasant. If we did not sometimes taste of adversity, prosperity would not be so welcome -Anne Bradstreet

Is it so small a thing--to have enjoy'd the sun--o have lived light in the spring--to have loved, to have thought, to have done? -Matthew Arnold

Spring comes: the flowers learn their colored shapes -Maria Konopnicka

In Like A Lion, Out Like A Lamb

When Spring arrives the robin doth rejoice as she brings food to her new-borns. The frosts of winter now quench the thirst of flowers pushing through a drably

painted landscape. Soon our Creator will refresh the earth with a magnificent palette of living color. The fragrance of that beauty captures our souls and we delight once again in this awesome cycle of life. -Linda LaTourelle ©

Autumn

Autumn is the bite of the harvest apple
-Christina Petrowsky

Autumn is a second spring, Where every leaf's a flower
-Albert Camus

Meadowlarks

Meadowlarks
give lusty cheers
when spring appears
when spring appears.

Buds and seeds
prick up their ears
and blades of grass
show eager spears.

And only icicles
weep tears
when spring appears
when spring appears
-Aileen Fisher

Spring Again

Spring again
Spring again
Spring again
Isn't it?
Buds on the branches
A breeze in the blue
And me without mittens
My sweater unbuttoned
A spring full of things
All before me to do.
-Karla Kuskin

• • • • • • • • • • • • • • •

OUT-OF-DOORS

The kids are out-of-doors once more;
The heavy leggins that they wore,
The winter caps that covered ears
Are put away, and no more tears
Are shed because they cannot go
Until they're bundled up just so.
No more she wonders when they're gone
If they have put their rubbers on;
No longer are they hourly told
To guard themselves against a cold;
Bareheaded now they romp and run
Warmed only by the kindly sun.
She's put their heavy clothes away
And turned the children out to play,
And all the morning long they race
Like madcaps round about the place.
The robins on the fences sing
A gayer song of welcoming,
And seems as though they had a share
In all the fun they're having there.
The wrens and sparrows twitter, too,
A louder and a noisier crew,
As though it pleased them all to see
The youngsters out of doors and free.
Outdoors they scamper to their play
With merry din the livelong day,
And hungrily they jostle in
The favor of the maid to win;
-continued on page 316

-continued from page 315

Then, armed with cookies or with cake,
Their way into the yard they make,
And every feathered playmate comes
To gather up his share of crumbs.
The finest garden that I know

is one where little
children grow,
Where cheeks
turn brown and
eyes are bright,
And all is laughter
and delight.
Oh, you may brag
of gardens fine,
But let the children
race in mine;

And let the roses, white and red,
Make gay the ground whereon they tread.
And who for bloom perfection seeks,
Should mark the color on their cheeks;
No music that the robin spouts
Is equal to their merry shouts;

There is no foliage to compare
With youngsters'
sun-kissed, tousled hair.

-Edgar Guest

316

It's Summer

"It's summer,"
Hum the bumblebees.
"It's summer,"
Trill the chickadees.
"It's summer,"
Chatter all the trees,
And bullfrogs
Croak along with these,
"It's summer,
Summer!

Summer!
"It's summer!"
All the roosters crow.
"It's summer,"
Chant the breezes low.
"It's summer,"
Says the fireflies' glow,
And I reply,
"I know!
I know!
It's summer!"

B.J. Lee

Winter Night

Blow, wind, blow!
Drift the flying snow!
Send it twirling, whirling overhead!
There's a bedroom in a tree,
Where, snug as snug can be,
The squirrel nests in his cozy bed.
Scold, wind, scold,
So bitter and so bold!
Shake the windows with your tap, tap, tap!
With half-shut, dreamy eyes
The drowsy baby lies,
Cuddled close in his mother's lap.

-Mary F. Butts

Seasons

Months (Excerpt)

To flowers of May,
And sunny June
Brings longest day;
In scorched July
The storm-clouds fly
Lightening-torn;
August bears corn,
September fruit
In rough October
Earth must disrobe her;
Stars fall and shoot
In keen November;
And night is long
And cold is strong
In bleak December.
-Christina Rosetti

Children and Snowflakes...

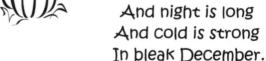

❄ No two are the same
❄ Each is unique in shape and size
❄ Alone they are fragile, but together, a force to be recognized
❄ They are fun to play with
❄ They melt in your arms
❄ They are a source of joy and wonder
❄ Pure and gentle

THE SNOW QUEEN

Where the wild bear clasps the ice
Over the hanging precipice,
Where the glittering icebergs shine
Within the sunset, red as wine,
Where the reindeer lick the snow,
To see what there may be below,
Where the shades are blue and green

There lives, they say,
the Great Snow Queen.
Wild her eyes are as the sea
When northern winds blow lustily.
Her queenly robes ar white as snow,
But flaming diamonds on them glow,
And many a precious stone.
Of green ice builded is her throne:
Polar bears her watch-dogs are—
Her only lamp, an evening star.
-Maud Keary

319

SHADOW

My Shadow

I have a little shadow that goes in and out with me,
And what can be the use of him is more than I can see.
He is very, very like me from the heels up to the head;
And I see him jump before me, when I jump into my bed.

The funniest thing about him is the way he likes to grow-
Not at all like proper children, which is always very slow;
For he sometimes shoots up taller, like an India-rubber ball,
And he sometimes gets so little that there's none of him at all.

He hasn't got a notion of how children ought to play,
And can only make a fool of me in every sort of way.
He stays so close beside me, he's a coward you can see;
I'd think shame to stick to nursie as that shadow sticks to me!

One morning, very early, before the sun was up,
I rose and found the shining dew on every buttercup;
But my lazy little shadow, like an arrant sleepyhead,
Had stayed at home behind me and was fast asleep in bed.
-Robert Louis Stevenson

SIBLINGS

My Little Sister

I have a little sister,
She's only two years old
But she's a little darling,
And worth her weight in gold.
She often runs to kiss me
When I'm at work or play,
Twining her arms about me
In such a pretty way.
And then she'll say so sweetly,
In innocence and joy,
"Tell me story, sister dear,
About the little boy."
Sometimes when I am knitting
She'll pull my needles out,
And then she'll
Skip and dance around
With such a merry shout.

Why?

My mom says I'm her sugarplum.
My mom says I'm her lamb.
My mom says I'm completely perfect
Just the way I am.
My mom says I'm a super-special,
wonderfully terrific little guy!
Mom just had another baby,
Why?

My pretty baby brother
Is six months old to-day,
And, though he cannot speak,
He knows whate'er I say.
Whenever I come near
He crows for very joy,
And dearly do I love him,
The darling baby-boy!

Oh, my dear, dear baby brother,
Our darling and our pet!
The very sweetest plaything
I ever have had yet.
The pretty little creature,
He grows so every day
That when the summer comes
In the garden he will play.
How cunning he will look
Among the grass and flowers!
No blossom is so fair
As this precious one of ours.
Every night before I sleep,
When I kneel to say my prayer,
I ask my heavenly Father
Of my brother to take care.

Sister
Sing me a song-
What shall I sing?
Three merry sisters
Dancing in a ring,
Light and fleet upon their feet.
As birds upon the wing.

♡

A sister ...

Is a forever friend
Is a special part of all that is
precious to my heart

❀

Close to my heart you'll always be
Friends from the start
I'll always do my best with my
sister by my side.

Memories of childhood may sometimes fade,
but never the special games we played.
Though our tea party days have come to an end,
You're always my sister, always my friend.

Simply Incredible sister
Sisters are blossoms in the garden of life.
Three things make life worth living...
God, sisters, and choc'lit cookies.
Best friends are we, my sister and me.

I love you little brother,
And you are fond of me;
Let us be kind to one another,
As brothers ought to be.
You shall learn to play with me,
And learn to use my toys;
And then I think that we shall be
Two happy little boys.
-Mother Goose

THE LITTLE BROTHER

Little brother in a cot,
Baby, baby!
Shall he have a pleasant lot?
Maybe, maybe!
Little brother in a nap,
Baby, baby!
Bless his tiny little cap,
Noise far away be!
With a rattle in his hand,
Baby, baby!
Dreaming—who can understand
Dreams like this, what they be?
When he wakes, kiss him twice,
Then talk and gay be;
Little cheeks soft and nice,
Baby, baby!
-Lilliput Levee

THE GOOD-NATURED GIRLS

Two good little children, named Mary and Ann,
Both happily live, as good girls always can;
And though they are not either sullen or mute,
They seldom or never are heard to dispute.
If one wants a thing that the other would like—
Well,—what do they do? Must they quarrel and strike?
No, each is so willing to give up her own,
That such disagreements are there never known.
If one of them happens to have something nice,
Directly she offers her sister a slice;
And never, like some greedy children, would try
To eat in a corner with nobody by!
When papa or mamma has a job to be done,
These good little children immediately run;
Nor dispute whether this or the other should go,
They would be ashamed to behave themselves so!
Whatever occurs, in their work or their play,
They are willing to yield, and give up their own way:
Then now let us try their example to mind,
And always, like them, be obliging and kind.

-Unknown

My Sister

Teddy bears, doll and dress up clothes,
The time went by so fast;
Tea parties filled with giggling frills,
Sweet memories from the past.
You were always there beside me,
As we grew up through the years;
You shared my sorrows and my joys,
My laughter and my tears.
There's something God has given me,
A gift so sweet and rare;
A love for my sister deep in my heart,
And a friend who will always be there.

-Allison Chambers Coxsey © (See Bio)

SICKNESS

MUM, I THINK I'VE GOT A COLD

Mum, I think I've got a cold
Or maybe it's the flu
I don't think I should go to school
I really don't, do you?
I'm sure I've got a temperature
My forehead feels quite hot
And if you look beneath my hair
I'm sure there's lots of spots
My skin feels very clamy
My hands are cold as ice
And the lump that's in my nostril
Just isn't very nice
So can I stay off school Mum?
To heal my aches and pains
Then if I feel OK next week
I'll go to school again

What's that you say? I'm going!!
You don't believe a word
You say that you are sceptical
Of all you've seen and heard
I know that I've got English Lit
Physics and PE
Latin, French and Metalwork
Maths and Chemistry
But I think you are mistaken
Your attitude is cruel
You stand with pointed finger saying
"Get yourself to school"
So I guess I'd better get my coat
Then tidy up my hair
But sending me on such a day
Just isn't very FAIR!!!!!
-Rob Erskine © (See Bio)

ANIMAL CRACKERS

Animal crackers and cocoa to drink,
That is the finest of suppers , I think;
When I am grown up and can have what I please,
I think I shall always insist upon these.

-Christopher Morley

CHICKEN POX SPOTS

Oh look at all my awful spots!
I must have the chicken pox.
They're on my arms and in my nose,
Between my fingers and even my toes.
They're in my ears and in my hair
These yucky pox are everywhere!
From head to foot and belly, too,
I itch so bad I might turn blue.
I pray that they will go away,
So I can go outside to play.

What are your special memories
Of someone caring for you when you were sick?
Did you have family traditions? Do you do the
same now with your children? Journal it for
them and for you to remember those special
times of tender loving care. It's comforting to
remember how much someone took care of you.

SINGLE PARENT

I know that, God, you've not ordained a family to be led by one. But there's no way to change the past or undo what has been done and so, Dear Lord, I come today for strength and guidance too. As I am a single parent and must depend solely on you. Please help me to develop the skills my child needs to observe in me. So that I can mend that tender heart and have peace within my family. Then help me squeeze in quality time to enjoy watching my child grow. Time to create lasting memories that come when love and happiness flow. When I'm feeling desperate or lonely, give me hope and grace to see that I never have been all alone.. For you've been right there with me!

-Dotty Barwick © (see bio)

Help me to lead my family with love!

Sleeping
Baby Asleep

Step lightly, for he sleeps! The tiny hands,
Restless and fluttering like a leaf wind-tossed
But scarce a moment since, might chiseled be
By sculptor's tool, so meekly are they crossed.
Rose-tinted palms and dimpled fingers white,
Lightly as snowflakes fall they passive lie,
Meet only for soft kisses. Little hands,
What burdens will life bring you by and by?
Speak softly, for he sleeps! Brown silken lashes fringe
The snowy curtains drooping low which hide
From baby's wondering eyes the strange new world
With all its pains and pleasures yet untried
Dear trustful eyes, within whose violet depths,
Where innocence is mirrored, never lies
A shadowed doubt of aught that life can bring,
For life to baby is one glad surprise.
Hush, for he sleeps! The dimpled, restless feet,
So tireless in their motion to and fro,
Are quiet now. Oh, tender baby feet,
With all life's toilsome journey yet to go,
You are so softly shielded from all harm
Yet not love's tenderest care can smooth the way
That lies before you in the great unknown,
Where with the sunlight lie the shadows gray.
Hush let him sleep! The rounded rose flushed cheek,
The parted lips curved in a happy smile
Are all the fairer for the peaceful rest
Which cannot be love-sheltered so erstwhile.
Sleep on, my baby, while I guard thy rest,
Thinking meantime upon the love that keeps
Over thy life more tender watch and ward
Than even mother's love. Hush, baby sleeps!
-Mrs. M E Paul

SWEET DREAMS

I gazed upon an Angel
Sleeping soundly in her bed.
As I watched her breathing,
Visions filled my head.
What degree of greatness
Lays in store for you?
Will you become a statesman
Or soar the skies of blue?
Perhaps, you'll dine with princes
Or a scholar you may be.
Will you save lives with healing
Or lead our world with wisdom?
For now your world is daddy's arms
And your mother's gentle touch.
You have changed so many lives
Because you're loved so much.
Sleep tight our little Angel,
Until the morning dew,
The problems of the world can wait
At least until your two!
-Barbara K. Cox © (See Bio)

Now I lay me down to sleep. I pray the Lord my soul to keep. God protect me all night long, and angels guard my bed.

Sleep Titles

- A Dream is a Wish Your Heart Makes
- A Lullaby Moment
- A New Day Is Dawning
- All I Have To Do Is Dream
- All Tucked In
- And to All a Good Night
- Are You Afraid of the Dark
- Arise from Your Sleep
- As I Lay Me Down to Sleep
- At Sleep and at Play
- Back to Sleep
- Beautiful Dreamer
- Boy, am I pooped
- Catching a Few Zzzzzz
- Caught Napping
- Close your little sleepy eyes . . .
- Counting Sheep
- Do Not Disturb
- Down for the Count
- Dream Painter
- Dream Sweet Dreams
- Dream Time
- Dream Weaver
- Dreamland Express
- Golden Slumbers
- Good Morning, America
- Good Morning, Merry Sunshine
- Good night Sweetheart
- Good Night, Moon
- Good night, sleep tight, don't let the bed bugs bite.
- Having a child fall asleep in your arms is one of the most peaceful feelings in the world.
- Hush Little Baby
- I am a Dream Come True
- I Don't Do Mornings
- If I'm not sleeping, nobody's sleeping
- I'll rise...but I refuse to shine

☆ I'm awake! Let's play!

☆ Lullaby & Good night

☆ Mama Tuck Me In

☆ Meet Me In My Dream

☆ Mr. Sandman

☆ My Angel... Only when he/she's sleeping

☆ Night Night little one

☆ Nightie, Night

☆ Now I Lay Me Down To Dream

☆ Now I lay me down to sleep

☆ Oh, How I Hate to Get Up in the Morning

☆ Only in My Dreams

☆ Our Little Sleeping Angel

☆ Rock-a-bye Baby

☆ Shhh...baby is dreaming

☆ Sleep Tight

☆ Sleep Tight, Sweet Prince

☆ Sleeping Beauty

☆ Sleepless in _____

☆ Sleepy time Gal/Guy

☆ Sweet Dreams are Made of This

☆ Sweet Slumber

☆ The Gift of Slumber

☆ The Princess of Dreams

☆ There is nothing so precious as a sleeping baby

☆ Things that Go Bump in the Night

☆ This Is How An Angel Sleeps

☆ Time for a Nap!

☆ Time for Bed, Sleepy Head

☆ To sleep, perchance to dream

☆ Wake Up Little Suzy

☆ Wake Up Sleepyhead

☆ When I Dream

☆ Zonked out

☆ Zzzzzz

Don't Wake the Baby

Baby sleeps so we must tread
Softly round her little bed,
And be careful that our toys
Do not fall and make a noise.
Play and talk, but whisper low;
Mother wants to work, we know,
That when father comes to tea
All may neat and cheerful be.

♡

Go to sleep, little baby;
When you awake
I'll give you a ginger cake,
And a whole lot of little horses;
One will be red,
One will be blue,
One will be the color of your mother's shoe!

As I stood and watched you sleeping
the moonlight kissed your face
My heart was overwhelmed
by your beauty and your grace
How precious and so delicate
is your tiny little hand
And the sweetness of your lips and eyes
is nothing less than grand.
Your spirit and your softness tenderly
sets my heart aglow
With a love so deep and infinite
that only a mother could know.
So tonight I count my blessings
for my darling, baby dear
For surely God did hear my heart
and answered every prayer. -Linda LaTourelle ©

In The Firelight

The fire upon the hearth is low,
And there is stillness everywhere,
And, like wing'd spirits, here and there
The firelight shadows fluttering go.
And as the shadows round me creep,
A childish treble breaks the gloom
And softly from a further room
Comes: "Now I lay me down to sleep."

And, somehow, with that little pray'r
And that sweet treble in my ears,
My thought goes back to distant years,
And lingers with a dear one there;
And as I hear my child's amen,
My mother's faith comes back to me—
Crouched at her side I seem to be,
And mother holds my hands again.

Oh, for an hour in that dear place—
Oh, for the peace of that dear time—
Oh, for that childish trust sublime—
Oh, for a glimpse of mother's face!
Yet, as the shadows round me creep,
I do not seem to be alone—
Sweet magic of that treble tone
And "Now I lay me down to sleep!"
-Eugene Field

Close your eyes baby
And listen to my sweet song
Sleep will come to thee all night long.

Slumber on, Baby dear;
Do not hear thy mother's sigh
Breathed for him far away,
While she sings thy lullaby!
Slumber on; o'er thy sleep
Loving eyes will watch with care;
In thy dreams may thou see
God's own angels hovering here.
-H.C. Watson

Sleepy Child

Sleepy trial,
Wipe your eyes
Yawn and squirm
And wiggle.

Fighting sleep
Nodding deep,
Heading off to
Count the sheep.

Bobbing head and
Slow deep breaths
As we carry you
To the bed.

Restless one
Slumber on for
The day is done,
And tomorrow there
Will be another.
-Shanda Purcell ©

The Sandman

Come, little girl, put by your things, the sand-man comes this way. He'll soon pass by and you and I will feel the spell he brings and say: Sleep till break of day. Dolly is sleepy: watch her head. The sand-man's on the way. She cannot sigh nor close her eye, She gives a nod instead to say: Sleep till break of day. Ah, there he goes! I caught him then as he came down this way. By yawn and sigh and sleepy eye I'd know his face again and say: Sleep till break of day.

-unknown

Sleep pretty baby and I will sing you a lullaby

Sleep, pretty baby,
The world awaits
Day with you;
Morning returns to
Us ever too soon.
Roses unfold, in
Their loveliness,
All for you;
Blossom the lilies
for hope of your glance.

Sleep my little babe
Sleep my precious soul;
Sleep all through the night
My little morning star.

Shut-Eye Town

Come my little one, with me!
There are wondrous sights to see
As the evening shadows fall;
In your pretty cap and gown,
Don't detain
The Shut-Eye train—
"Ting-a-ling!" the bell goeth,
"Toot-toot!" the whistle bloweth,
And we hear the warning call:
"All aboard for Shut-Eye Town!"
Over hill and over plain
Soon will speed the Shut-Eye train!
Through the blue where bloom the stars
And The Mother Moon looks down
We'll away to land of Fay---
Oh, the sights that we shall see there!
Come my little one, with me there—
'T is goodly train of cars—
All aboard for Shut-Eye Town!
Swifter than a wild bird's flight,
Through the realms of fleecy light
We shall speed and speed away!
Let the Night in envy frown—
What care we how wroth she be!
To the Balow-land above us,
To the Balow-fold who love us,
Let us hasten while we may---
All aboard for Shut-Eye Town!

Shut-Eye Town is passing fair—
Golden dreams await us
there;
We shall dream those dreams,
my dear, till the Mother
Moon goes down—See un-
fold delights untold!
-Eugene Field

• • • • • • • • • • • • • • • •

THE SILVER BOAT

There is a boat upon the sea'
It never stops for you or me,
The sea is blue, the boat is white,
It sails through winter and summer night.
The swarthy child in India land
Points to the prow with eager hand;
The little Lapland babies cry
For the silver boat a-sailing by.
It fears no gale, it fears no wreck,
It neer meets a change or check
Through weather fair or weather wild;
The oldest saw it when a child.
Upon another sea below
Full many vessels come and go;
Upon the swaying, swinging tide
Into the distant worlds they ride.
And, strange to tell, the sea below,
Where countless vessels come and go,
Obeys the little boat on high
Through all the centuries sailing by.
-Mrs. M.F. Butts

Come now, dear children, come and eat,
Your pudding's hot, your milk is sweet.
Then quietly retire up stairs,
With grateful hearts, and fervent prayers;
Undress, and go to bed and sleep,
Till morning light begins to peep.
-A Lady of Boston

When the busy day is done,
And my weary lttle one
Rocketh gently to and fro;
When the night winds softly blow,
Through the murk and mist and gloom,
To our quiet, cozy home,
Where to singing, sweet and low,
Rocks a cradle to and fro;
Where the clock's dull monotone
Telleth of the day that's done;
where the moonbeams hover o'er
Plaything sleeping on the floor-
Where my weary wee one lies
Cometh Lady Button Eyes.
Fairies dance around their queen
Then from yonder misty skies
Cometh Lady Button-Eyes.
-Eugene Field

♡

There is nothing sweeter
Than sleeping with your babies
And, feeling their breath
On your cheeks.

♡

Sleep, my baby, on my bosom,
warm and cozy it will prove.
Round thee mother's arms are folding
In her heart a mother's love.

♡

Dream Sweet Dreams

• • • • • • • • • • • • • • • •

Hush Little Child

Hush little child,
whimpering in dreams
your all cozy and warm,
wrapped in rainbows
and moonbeams
outside the wind howls,
there's frost on the ground
And Autumn is whining,
its early warning sound
so hush my baby,
there's no cause for alarm
for in your life,
you'll face many a storm
But with God at your side,
there is nothing to fear
Because his love and affection,
will always be near.

-Michael Levy © (See Bio)

THE ROCK-A-BY LADY

The Rock-a-by Lady from Hush-a-by Street
Comes stealing, comes creeping;
The poppies they hang from her head to her feet
And each hath a dream that is tiny and fleet,
She bringeth her poppies to you, my sweet,
When she finds you sleeping!
So shut the tow eyes that are weary, my sweet,
For the Rock-a-by Lady from Hush-a-by Street,
With poppies that hang from her head to her feet,
Comes stealing, comes creeping. —Eugene Field

THE LITTLE DREAMER

A little boy was dreaming,
Upon his nurse's lap.
That the pins fell out of all the stars
And the stars fell into his cap.
So, when his dream was over,
What should that little boy do?
Why, he went and looked inside his cap.
And found it wasn't true.
-Nursery Nonsense

Sleep, my baby, on my breast
Warm and cozy softly rest
Mama's arms will safely keep thee
All the while you dream so sweetly.
-Linda LaTourelle ©

Sleep, baby, sleep
Your father tends the sheep
Your mother shakes the dreamland tree
And from it fall sweet dreams for thee.

• • • • • • • • • • • • • • •

OH, LITTLE CHILD

Hush, little one, and fold your hands—
The sun hath set, the moon is high;
The sea is singing to the sands,
And wakeful posies are beguiled
By many a fairy lullaby—
Hush, little child—my little child!

Dream, little one, and in your dreams
Float upward from this lowly place—
Float out on mellow, misty streams
To lands where bideth Mary mild,
And let her kiss thy little face,
You little child—my little child!

Sleep, little one, and take thy rest—
With angels bending over thee,
Sleep sweetly on that Father's breast
Whom our dear Christ hath reconciled—
But stay not there—come back to me,
Oh, little child—my little child!

-Eugene Fields

The nicest dreams
that will ever be
are the dreams shared
by my teddy and me.

HYMN OF A CHILD

Loving Jesus, meek and mild,
Look upon a little child!
Make me gentle as Thou art,
Come and live within my heart.
Take my childish hand in thine,
Guide these little feet of mine.
So shall all my happy days
Sing their pleasant song of praise;
And the world shall always see
Christ, the holy Child, in me!
-abridged from C. Wesley

BABY MINE

Baby mine, over the trees
Baby mine, over the flowers;
Baby mine, over the sushine;
Baby mine, over the showers.
Baby mine, over the land;
Baby mine, over the water.
Oh, when I had a mother before
Such a sweet
Such a sweet,
blessed child!

SMILE

What would you take for that smile in the morn,
Those bright, dancing eyes and the face they adorn;
For the sweet little voice that you hear all day
Laughing and cooing-yet nothing to say?

COME, MY LITTLE CHILDREN

Come, my little children, here are songs for you;
Some are short and some are long and all, are new.
You must learn to sing them very small and clear,
Very true to time and tune and pleasing to the ear.
Mark the note that rises, mark the notes that fall.
Mark the time when broken, and the swing of it all.
So when night is come and you have gone to be,
All the songs you love to sing shall echo in your
head. -Robert Louis Stevenson

I'll keep you right here in my
heart And I'll memorize
every little part

SANDWICHES

Sandwiches are beautiful,
Sandwiches are fine.
I like sandwiches,
I eat them all the time;
I eat them for my supper,
And I eat them for lunch;
If I had a hundred sandwiches,
I'd eat them all at once.

Michael, row
your boat
ashore,
Hallelujah.
Michael, row
your boat
ashore,
Hallelujah!

MOTHER'S SWEETEST SONG

The first time that she held me,
Was underneath her heart;'
God placed me there to feel her love,
Right from the very starts.
The first time ti heard a lullaby,
Her voice, so soft and warm;
In that haven of peace and slumber,
Nestled safely in arms.
It was the sweetest melody,
Of love that lingers long;
The lullaby she sang to me,
Was my Mother's sweetest song.
Then as I went through childhood,
Her wisdom helped me grow;
A mother's love to guide me,
To learn what I should know.
Looking back I wonder,
Was there a time she wasn't there?
No matter where life led me,
I was in my Mother's prayers.
Now winger winds blow softly,
'Cross love that lingers long;
In the beauty of the memory,
Of my Mother's sweetest song.

-Allison Chambers Coxsey © (See Bio)

• • • • • • • • • • • • • • • • • • •

DADDY'S FAVORITE SONG

There was a time so long ago,
She stood on Daddy's feet;
Her head tipped back, she laughed at him,
With a childish voice so sweet.

They whirled & swirled, they dipped & swayed,
The music played on and on;
But the melody of her laughter,
Was her Daddy's favorite song.

She climbed into her Daddy's lap,
To rest there in his arms;
Her head tucked there beneath his chin,
A bundle sweet and warm.

Her head would nod, her eyes would droop,
As she lay there on his chest;
The safety of his loving arms,
Brought peaceful, slumbering rest.

Those days have passed, the years have dimmed,
But memories are not gone;
Of the little girl on her Daddy's feet,
Dancing to his favorite song.
    -Allison Chambers Coxsey ©1996 (See Bio)

You are Daddy's little girl
And Mommy's precious babe
No one could love you more
Than your parent's for their child

Sweet Child of Mine, I Love You So
May your days be blessed forever more

BABY SONG

Little babe with eyes of blue,
Heaven must have smiled on you;
The day God formed you in His hand,
He had for you a special plan.

To give His gift of joy and love,
He sent an angel from above;
His hand caressed your tiny face,
To fill you with His love and grace.

Then when His laughter filled the air,
He touched your heart and placed it there;
The sweetest part of God's own soul,
He poured in you to make you whole.

Then He bade the angels come,
To see the gift was almost done;
Sweet lullabies then filled the air,
For the tiny angel slumbering there.

As angels leaned to kiss your face,
Two dimples formed to take their place;
While crystal angel's voices ring,
Your gold curls formed like angel's wings.

Tears fell from the angel's eyes,
As one by one they said goodbye;
For God would send you down to earth,
A gift from Heaven at your birth.

Little babe with eyes of blue,
God's sweetest gift was sending you.

-Allison Chambers Coxsey
©1996 (See Bio)

Sorrow and Loss

ANGEL KISSES, MY SON

In another happy lifetime to come,
I know that you will get to run,
Playing baseball with the other boys.
A bright sunny time filled with joys.
Seeing you gasping for each breath,
A weakened shell of your old self.
No longer able to lift up your head.
Just skin and bones lie upon the bed.
The Oncologist's diagnosis was so bleak.
Time left, minutes, not another week.
Death for you will finally bring
Release from suffering.
You will know such sweet peace.
Slowly your closed eyes open wide.
Once more I am so filled with pride.
The Lord has come to take you Home.
A radiant smile lingers. You are gone.
Angel Kisses, my beloved son.

-Lottie Ann Knox © (See Bio)

Jesus Loves You
He will care
For you always
He is there

SORROW AND LOSS

In a land for babies, just beyond my eye
My darling plays with angel toys that money doesn't buy
Who am I to wish her back into this world of strife?
No, play on my baby, you have eternal life.
At night when all is silent and sleep forsakes my eyes,
I'll hear her tiny footsteps come running to my side.
Her little hands caress me so tenderly and sweet,
I'll breathe a prayer and close my eyes
and embrace her in my sleep.
No, I have a treasure I rate above the other,
I have known true glory— I am still her mother.
-Unknown

MY DAUGHTER

All the dreams I prayed you'd be
Are all the things you are.
You were once my little girl
And now my shining star.

Born, still to us, but alive to God!
No sorrow, but everlasting peace,
So separation, but communion forever
...with God.

You will probably feel very lonely in your grief.
No one else knew your baby except you,
—the parents.
Others will soon forget.
You will continue to remember your child's
Impact on your life.

OUR LITTLE QUEEN

Could you have seen the violets
That blossomed in her eyes;
Could you have kissed that golden hair,
And drank those holy sights;
You would have been her tiring maid
As joyfully as I,--
Content to dress your little queen,
And let the world go by.
Could you have seen those violets
Hide in their graves of snow;
Drawn all that gold along your hand
While she lay smiling so;--
O, you would tread this weary earth
As heavily as I!—
Content to clasp her little grave,
And let the world go by.

-Overland Monthly

It Is Well With My Soul

When peace, like a river,
attendeth my way,
When sorrows like sea billows roll;
Whatever my lot,
Thou has taught me to say,
It is well, it is well, with my soul.

SPORTS

BASEBALL

The pitcher is ready; he pulls his arm back,
And sends the bar hurling my way.
But if he was hoping for me to strike out,
Then I guess this just isn't his day.
I swing-and the sound as the bat hits the ball,
Is like thunder that makes the earth quake;
And the ball is a rocket that roars out of sight
As the pitcher regrets his mistake.
I jog 'round the bases, giving everyone five
and though this is only a dream;
I promise that's just what would happen today
If only you'd pick me for your team.

-Joe Thompson © (See Bio)

BASKETBALL

I Love to play ball

I love to play with my ball.
I love to bounce it most of all
I love to play in the sun.
I love to catch the ball and run!
I love to find a basket hoop
I love to dribble and to shoot.
And the most fun of all,
I s having my friends to come play ball!

-Thena Smith ©

352

Play Ball With Me

Daddy, come play ball with me
While the sun is out
I can catch the ball
I know that without a doubt!
Daddy come and play ball with me
Let's shoot a hoop or two!
I am getting taller now
And I can make a basket too!
Daddy come and play with me
Let's, shoot or toss or catch the ball
For just being with you, Daddy
Is the most fun of all!
-Thena Smith ©

- A grand slam
- Backyard soccer
- Backyard baseball
- Batter up
- Casey at the bat
- Double play
- Field of dreams
- Fly ball
- Gliding light
- Goal!
- Going...going...gone
- Havin' a ball
- Heart of a champion
- Hero worship
- Hey batter batter
- Hitting the ice
- Homerun!
- I get a kick out of soccer
- League all your own
- Instant replay
- Kick back and have a great time!
- Let the games begin
- Little big league
- Little slugger
- Little sport
- Major league fun
- Mvp
- My goal is to play soccer
- Angels in the outfield
- No pain, no gain
- No! The other way!
- Pitching in
- Play ball
- Player down...
- Prime time sports
- Ready, set, goal!
- Rookie of the year
- Root root root for the home team
- Score!
- Seventh-inning stretch
- Ski bum
- Slapshot
- Sledding buddies
- Sleigh ride
- Slip and slide
- Slippin' and slidin'
- Soccer Dad
- Soccer is a kick
- Soccer mom
- Soccer season
- Soccer's a ball!
- Sports superstar
- Stealing second
- Steeeerike!
- Step up to the plate
- Take me out to the ball game
- Taste of victory
- The agony of defeat
- The last hit
- The puck drops here
- The puck stops here
- The rookie
- The sports page
- The sweet smell of victory
- Three strikes, you're out
- Today's heroes
- Triple play
- What a kick!
- Winning with style
- World series here we come
- You're out

Step Family

That it might in the will of sunlight sing
So may we long remain through love and art
Stepparent and Stepchildren of the heart.

We are a family now, a whole,
Of which you are a part,
And you are just as much my child
As any in my heart.
I don not love you differently,
Nor would I give up less
Of all that life has given me
To bring you happiness
There is no limit to my love,
No boundary you might cross,
No price you might be asked to pay,
No need to fear its loss.
We are now one, the four of us,
Windows of hone home
As long as I have life and breath,
You'll never be alone.

Talking/Walking

THE CHATTERBOX
From morning till night it was Lucy's delight
To chatter and talk without stopping;
There was not a day but she rattled away,
Like water for ever a-dropping.
No matter at all if the subjects were small,
Or not worth the trouble of saying,
'Twas equal to her, she would talking prefer
To working, or reading, or playing.
-Unknown

SUN, MOON & STARS

- A star is born!
- Baby, I'm a star!
- Celestial bliss
- Fun in the sun
- Galaxy quest
- Goodnight moon
- Magic moon
- Moonlight madness
- Moonlight serenade
- Moonstruck
- Reach for the stars
- Shooting star
- Under the stars
- Walkin' on sunshine
- Wish upon a star
- You are my sunshine
- Stars in their eyes
- Swinging on a star
- The skies the limit
- Interplanetary craft!
- My daddy hung the moon
- Good morning sonshine
- By the light of the silvery moon
- The sun'll come out tomorrow

I see the moon
The moon sees me
The moon sees the one
I long to see.
God bless the moon
And God bless me
And God bless the one
I long to see.

The man in the moon
Looked out of the moon
And this is what he said,
'Tis time that, now I'm
Getting up,
All babies went to bed.

I see the moon,
The moon sees me.
God bless the moon,
And God bless me.

Twinkle, Twinkle
Little Star
Like the Diamond
that you are.

Star light, star bright
First star I've seen tonight
Wish I may, wish I might
Have the wish, I wish tonight.

THE LITTLE DREAMER
A little boy was dreaming,
Upon his nurse's lap,
That the pins fell out of all the stars,
And the stars fell into his cap.
So, when his dream was over,
What should that little boy do?
Why, he went and looked inside his cap,
And found it wasn't true.
-Nursery Nonsense

Little Girlie
Little girlie tell to me
What your wistful blue eyes see/
Why you like to stand so high,
Looking at the far off sky.
Does a tiny Fairy flit
In the pretty blue of it?
Or is it that you hope so soon
To see the rising yellow moon?

SUN, MOON & STARS

WHO BLOWS YOU OUT

O little round and yellow moon,
Why have you lit yourself so soon?
Jane won't bring in the lamp for me,
She says it's light enough to see!
Perhaps you did not know the time,
But don't you hear the church clocks chime?
Who blows you out, I wonder, when
The shining day comes back again?

Baby's fishing for a dream,
Fishing near and far,
His line a silver moonbeam is,
His bait a silver star.
-Alice Riley

MOTHER MOON AND STARS

The moon is bending o'er the sea,
As I my babe, bend over thee;
She rocks it gently to and fro,
As I now rock you—so, and so;
The wind, her breath, sings softly,
"Dear, sleep sweetly, now, for I am near."
The stars look down upon the lea,
As I, my babe, look down on thee;
The earth's at rest; They vigils keep,
As I watch o'er thy peaceful sleep,
And through the silence I can hear,
"Sleep sweetly now, for we are near."

358

Sweetness

One small hand to hold in yours,
One small face to smile,
One sweet kiss good night
one small child to love.
Treasure the moment
The years too soon will fly.
These are precious moments,
More than money can buy.
Treasure the moment
Put it in your heart
Forever more.

SWINGING

Swing me up and swing me down,
Swing me up towards the sky—
Swinging is like being blown,
Blow me up and let me fly,
Like a piece of thistle-down—
Swing me up towards the sky!

Up, up in the air
Flying so free and so fast
Touching the sky
Fast as I fly
Swinging away
Happy today!

· · · · · · · · · · · · · · · · · ·

SWINGING SONG

A hammock gently swinging,
A mother bends above;
She to her babe is singing
With heart all full of love.
The little maiden swaying
Beneath the greenwood tree
Has set her heart to saying,
"Love me as I love thee."
So swaying, swinging slowly,
Her loved one to and fro,
Her heart with rapture holy
Out to her baby doth go;
And while her thoughts are straying
Among the days to be,
Her heart is ever saying,
"Love me as I love thee."
How do you like to go up in a swing,
Up in the air so blue?
Oh, I do think it the pleasantest thing
Ever a child can do!

The Swing

Up in the air and over the wall,
Till I can see so wide,
Rivers and trees and cattle and all
Over the countryside—

Till I look down on the garden green,
Down on the roof so brown—
Up in the air I go flying again,
Up in the air and down!
-Robert Louis Stevenson

360

My teddy, my best friend
Beary Wuvable

Here sits my teddy bear, all tattered and torn.
Everybody loves him even though he's so worn.

His body is floppy, his hair is a mess.
But I love him dearly and he loves me
best.

Fuzzy Wuzzy was a bear
Fuzzy Wuzzy had no hair
Fuzzy Wuzzy wasn't fuzzy, was he?

Little hearts never fear, when teddy bears are near.

Bears do not like to be lent. Save to very small children in very great distress. -Helen Thomson

Wake in the deepest dark of night and hear the driving rain. Reach out a hand and take a paw and go to sleep again. -Charlotte Gray

Teddy bears are stuffed with dreams and memories.

Here sits my teddy bear, all tattered and torn.
Everybody loves him even though he's so worn.
His body is floppy, his hair is a mess.
But I love him dearly and he loves me best.

The nicest dreams that will ever be
are the dreams shared by my teddy and me.

TEDDY Bear. Teddy Bear. turn out the light.
Teddy Bear. Teddy Bear. say good night.

Teeth

- ☺ A Pool of Drool
- ☺ A Time To Brush
- ☺ A Tooth in the Hand
- ☺ First tooth
- ☺ Look Mom, No Cavities
- ☺ Look Mom, No Teeth
- ☺ Looth Tooth
- ☺ Lost All Wisdom
- ☺ Metal Mouth
- ☺ Pearly Whites
- ☺ Teething is terrible
- ☺ The Tooth Fairy was Here
- ☺ Tooth or Consequences
- ☺ Toothless Wonder
- ☺ Train Tracks
- ☺ Wiggle it, pull it, wrap it up tight..
- ☺ You don't have to brush all your teeth, just the ones you want to keep!
- ☺ All I Want for Christmas is My Two Front Teeth

THE TOOTH FAIRY

She came last night
And vanished away...
With the tooth
I pulled out
yesterday.
If I could follow,
I bet I'd spy...
A mountain
of teeth
That would
touch the sky!

I'VE LOST MY TWO FRONT TEETH

I've just lost my two front teeth
Now there's just a hole
They come out during bedtime
I was chewing a cheese roll
My friends all come and ask me
Can we have a peek
Mum says that it's lucky
The school photo was last week.
But I don't care about the gap
Just one thing makes me bristle
It's when I talk to anyone
It comes out with a whistle.

THE TOOTH FAIRY

When the tooth fairy heard you lost your tooth,
Do you know what she did?
She made a map to visit you,
'Cause you're a special kid!
First she got your home address
And checked her fairy map.
Then she flew to your place
Where she saw your brand new "gap"
Of course, she took your worn-out tooth
Just like she's always done.
But she's left you something nice instead
To help you have some fun!

A TOOTH FELL OUT

A tooth fell out and left a space
So big, my tongue can touch my face.
And every time I smile, I show
A space where something used to grow.
I miss my tooth as you may guess,
But then I have to brush one less

TIME

THREE FEET TALL

Mischief in a package,
That stands just three feet tall;
A power - packed bundle of energy,
In a boy who is so small.

Competing with the Universe,
In a race against all time;
Curiosity follows hand in hand,
As they see what they can find.
An endless stream of chatter,
Pours forth without an end;
While new and fun adventures,
Wait just around the bend.

Only little just this once,
This bundle, three feet tall;
A treasure trove of life and joy,
In a boy who is so small.
-Allison Chambers Coxsey ©

ONE! TWO! THREE!

What a kidnapper Time can be!
He's stolen my little child away
That spoke my name but yesterday.
"Take all that I have of silver and gold,
And give me again little Two-Years-Old"—
Such reward I had offered you, and to you,
In beautiful year of Two.

Toddlers

When god made the motor for toddlers,
There's one thing He forgot, I fear.
Often, the throttle gets stuck on high,
For He forgot to include low gear.

Toddler's Greed

If I want it, it's mine.
If I give it to you, and change my mind later, it's mine.
If I take it away from you, it's mine.
If I had it a little while ago, it's mine.
If it's mine, it will never belong to anyone else, no matter what.
If we are building something together, all the pieces are mine.
If it looks just like mine, it is mine.

It's Mine

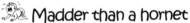 Kicking and screaming

 Madder than a hornet

 Major hissyfit

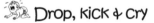 Waaaaaa

Drop, kick & cry

I want...

The Tantrum

Mommy calls it a tantrum
Papa calls it a fit. Daddy
calls it a disgrace and just
tells me to quit!

Grandma calls it a bid for
attention and holds me on
her knee. Sis calls it a
commotion and tries to
strangle me!

I call it necessary to get
attention to my woe
for when I get unhappy...
I think everyone should know!
-Thena Smith ©

365

Transportation

- 🚜 _____ the Builder
- 🚜 All Roads Lead to Home
- 🚜 And, Their Off!
- 🚜 Asleep At the Wheel
- 🚜 Baby Bumpers
- 🚜 Baling Hay
- 🚜 Big Green Machine
- 🚜 Big Wheels Keep on Rolling
- 🚜 Burning Rubber
- 🚜 Choo-Choo Man
- 🚜 Chugga-Chugga, Choo-Choo
- 🚜 Construction Zone
- 🚜 Cruising
- 🚜 Danger: Crew At Work
- 🚜 Demolition Derby
- 🚜 Demolition Zone
- 🚜 Diggin' in the Dirt
- 🚜 Discing Dude
- 🚜 Do the Loco-Motion
- 🚜 Down By the Station
- 🚜 Drive 'till You Drop
- 🚜 Driving Forces
- 🚜 Driving My Life Away
- 🚜 Driving With Your Eyes Closed
- 🚜 Dump truck buddies
- 🚜 Dump truck dudes
- 🚜 Filler' Up
- 🚜 Fly the Friendly Skies
- 🚜 Flying High
- 🚜 Four on the Floor
- 🚜 Full Throttle
- 🚜 Gas & Go
- 🚜 Good to Go
- 🚜 Goodbye Trike, Hello Bike
- 🚜 Got Dirt?
- 🚜 Got Mud?
- 🚜 Hard Hat Honey
- 🚜 Hauling a Load
- 🚜 Homeward Bound
- 🚜 Hot rod
- 🚜 Hot Wheels
- 🚜 I'm a Little Airplane Now
- 🚜 I'm a Little Choo-Choo
- 🚜 I'm Out of Here
- 🚜 If You Don't Like My Driving, Call 1-800-DadsBoy
- 🚜 Get Off the Road

- If You Don't Like My Driving; Get Off the Sidewalk
- Just Like Dad
- Let the Good Times Roll
- Little Engineer
- Little Man
- Look at me go
- Look Out!
- Making Hay While the Sun Still Shines
- My Little Chauffer
- One Lap to Go
- Pedal Pushers
- Pit Stop
- Planes, Trains, & Automobiles
- Plow Boy
- Put the Peddle to the Metal!
- Ready, Set, Go
- Red Light; Green Light
- Rocket Man
- She's on a Roll
- Tailgating
- Three Wheeling

- Ticket to Ride
- Tractor Pull
- Traffic Cop
- Truck Driving Man
- Trucking Toddler
- Two Tickets to Paradise
- Two Wheeling
- Up, Up, Up and Away
- Vroom-Vroom baby
- Zoom, Zoom, Zoom!
- 0 to 60 in 5 seconds
- Can't drive 55
- Speed trap
- 10-4 Good Buddy
- What's Your Handle?
- Loose Caboose
- Dump A Load
- Ride of My Life
- Got the Top Down & the Wind in My Hair
- Born to Ride
- Got Your Ears on Good Buddy
- Little Red Corvette
- Fully Charged & Ready to Go

Twins

- 2 hot 2 handle
- 2 is better than 1
- A double blessing
- All babies are terrific,
- And then there were 2
- Army of two
- Birds of a feather
- Blessings 2 by 2
- Denim duo
- Double duty
- Double take
- Double trouble
- Double your fun
- Double your pleasure
- Doubly blessed
- Dynamic duo
- Experience wildlife Have twins
- It takes two
- Me and my womb-mate
- Paired up
- Peas in a pod
- Seeing double
- Terrific triplets
- The more, the merrier
- Then there were two
- Trouble times two
- Twice as fun
- Twice as much fun
- Twice as much love
- Twice as nice
- Twice as special
- Twice blessed
- Twice the fun
- Two by two
- Two cute
- Two is better than one
- Two of a kind
- Two peas in a pod
- Two-rrific
- What a pair!

Twins

Two to get up
Two to play
Two to pick up
Two to pray
Double the work
But double the fun
Worth every minute
When day is done
♡♡

Two miracles instead of one
Two special lives have just begun
Two times the joy,
Two times the fun!
♡♡

I have two to sing to, two to cling to,
two to have each other.
And two to give for, two to live for ,
And twins to call me mother.
♡♡

One plus one is two
and that's the both of you.
Twice as much to love
two blessings from above.
God touched our hearts
so deep inside,
our special blessing
multiplied!

Totally 2-riffic

Walking

- Baby Steps
- Caution Kids Crossing
- Come to Momma
- First Steps
- I Saw Her Standing There
- Just a Closer Walk With Thee
- Little by Little, One Walks Far
- Look What I Do!
- Moon-walking
- One Step At a Time
- Put One Foot in Front of the Other
- The Journey Begins With a Single Step
- These Booties are Made For Walking
- These Feet Were Made for Walking
- Toddler Two Step
- Upward Mobility
- Walk of Life
- Walk the Talk
- Walking in Memphis
- Walking in the Rain
- Walking on Broadway
- Walking on Sunshine

Don't let your miracles become mundane. Don't let the miracle of your child become a burden. Don't let the miracles in your life become so common place that you don't even recognize them anymore. Don't take for granted what once was a miracle. Life is a miracle everyday!

Michael Levy was born in Manchester, England on March 6, 1945. After many life experiences and a successful business career he retired to Florida in 1992. In 1998 Michael established Point of Life, Inc. to project his philosophy and spiritual understanding. In just a few years he has become a world renowned poet.

His website and associated newsletter are visited and read by thousands of people around the world every month. Michael is also a frequent speaker on radio and television programs. And, he is a host on Voice America.com radio and Point of Life Show at Radio America. He also holds frequent seminars where he shares and discusses his views.

A member of the Templeton, Michael is the author of four books, and his essays grace many web sites, journals, and magazines throughout the world. More information on Michael Levy can be found on his website at: *http://www.pointoflife.com*

Rob Erskine lives in the United Kingdom with his wife and two daughters, ages 5 and 9. He is the manager in an organization that works with facilitating adults with special needs to learn to live independently. His hobbies include golf, fishing, and playing guitar.

His writing began as a gift to his daughters. On sleepless nights he would recite his poems to help them into slumber-land. More of his endearing poetry can be found on his website at *www.postpoems.com/members/camlann*.

Tom Krause is the author of *Touching Hearts-Teaching Greatness, Stories From A Coach That Touch Your Heart & Inspire Your Soul,* Andrews McMeel Publishing. He is also a International Motivational Speaker whose poetry has been read by over 3 million people world wide. He currently lives in Nixa, MO with his wife, Amy and sons, Tyler & Sam. Contact: *www.coachkrause.com*

Todd Jones This is the man! He's the best graphic designer ever! I am so delighted to share his talents with you. He has created awesome covers for each of our books, as well as, those attention getting ads in your favorite magazines. He is quick with his incredible imagination. And to top it off, he's a great bass guitar player, married to a real sweetheart. Together they have a little piece of paradise and they are raising a wonderful family and homeschool their children, too. It's a humbling experience to know him, because the joy of the Lord is truly a part of who he is. I am so thankful for his encouragement, friendship and awesome talent. What can I say, Todd. You're the best! (and Cindy, too!) Thanks for every little detail you're so good at recognizing and caring about. You are a blessing beyond compare. Much love and prayers.

Lettering Delights ... for awesome looking fonts that will make your layouts and other projects zing with creative genius. Be sure to visit this wonderful website and stock up on the best fonts you'll find. It's a user friendly website, designed so that you can not only preview these great fonts, but you can download them immediately for a nominal fee. Or, if you're a font addict, like I am, you'll want to have them all on CDs for easy access. I have been using their font creations for years now and love how they're always coming up with fun, new fonts. They're a terrific company with super customer service. Also, every month they have contests and a chance to win free fonts. They've even got a freebie section and newsletter. So, have a visit and expand your font horizons! *www.LetteringDelights.com*

Sandra Prouse was born in a small town in Pennsylvania and traveled the United States for 20 years as a military wife. She and her husband are the proud parents of three sons and three daughters.   They now reside in Port Orange, FL. Her poetry is inspired by her many travels, those she meets, her love for children, and her family. Her first book The Softest Kind of Love was well received and her second book, a children's book, is anticipated by her many fans. More of her poems at: *www.geocities.com/poetry/bysand/enchantedland.htm.*

Shanda Purcell is new to my business, and my life, but definitely part of a much bigger plan. God's timing is so perfect and I am so blessed to share this adventure with you, my partner. For all you have done in such a short amount of time, what can I say...pretty amazing, girl! Thanks for being the balance in this fun journey. You are a blessing in so many ways. Isn't it so exciting to watch our business grow? What a team! The sky's the limit and I can't wait to watch as dreams come true for us and others, that God intends, because of this business. I want you to know how much I appreciate you and how thankful I am to call you friend!

Nicholas Gordon, born on August 24, 1940, in Albany, New York, now lives in Fort Lee, New Jersey. He is married and has three children. He earned a B.A. in English from Queens College, an M.A. and Ph.D from Stanford University. He taught English at New Jersey City University, as well as other colleges and universities. Currently, he is retired from teaching, but has an active website that generates thousands of hits per day. His website is a collaboration of several hundred works from the last fifteen years. *www.poemsforfree.com*

In his own words...

"What I enjoy most about writing is the sense of overwhelming beauty that comes when something I have written seems, at least momentarily, to be precisely right. I love to read beautiful poems and novels, see beautiful paintings, and hear beautiful music, but there is an experience that comes from creating something myself that seems beautiful and is like nothing else."
-Nicholas Gordon

Loree Mason O'Neil was born on December 7, 1935, in the tiny town of Driftwood, Oklahoma which is located just south of the OK/KS state line. Her parents were dairy farmers. Aspiring to be a writer, Loree took two years of journalism while in high school. After graduation, she married and had four sons. As things go, she put her writing on hold.

However, in 2000 a greeting card site out of Canada posted one of Loree's older poems. It was well received, and the site owner asked if she had any more poems. At that point she says she started pumping them out. Loree learned that she truly enjoyed sharing her thoughts and experiences through poetry. In February of 2002, Loree published her first book of poetry: *All Roads Lead to Home*. She is also the author of four country/western and gospel songs. Another song, written especially for the recording artist, *Blinded by Love* is being promoted in England. *www.poetrybyloree.com*

S.E. Chan holds a degree in Theology and Pastoral Ministries with a focus in missionary work. As the single parent of three girls, she worked for many years with disadvantaged children and single-parents. Through her work she has gained a special interest in THE FOUNDATION FOR MISSING AND EXPLOITED CHILDREN. She asks that, "those who enjoy my poetry about family and kids, make a donation to that charity so that those who have missing kids might again be able, to one day, to hear the whispers of love that their children have for them."

Cool Baby Graphics Thanks for your contribution to this book. The founder and designer, Colleen Bouchard, started out designing a website for her cat, and things took off from there. She offers thematic designs for all occasions. More of these delightful graphics can be found at *www.coolbabygraphics.com*.

Thena Smith was born in a tiny farming community in western Kentucky where she remained until she married her college sweetheart in 1965. For the last 20 years she has lived in Coronado California with her husband Ron and her daughter Melissa.

Thena remembers writing her first poem at the age of 7 for a class Christmas project. Her mom sent it to the local newspaper and it was published. For many years, she wrote, but failed to save her writings. Finally encouraged by a friend to save her work, they presented a collage of poetry and music that was televised on a local cable station. She also co-wrote a children's musical that was presented locally.

Thena has always been a scrapper. And, as the hobby began to catch on she began to share verses with others. A local on the scrap-booking message boards, Thena has written hundreds of poems and shared them with her friends.

More of Thena's original writings can be found in her upcoming book "Where's Thena... I Need a Poem About..." You can buy her book at *www.theultimateword.com*

Allison Chambers Coxsey lives with her husband of over three decades, Ralph Coxsey, on the Gulf Coast of Mississippi. They moved to Mississippi after more than thirty years of living in Oklahoma. They are the proud parents of three adult children and have been blessed with two beautiful grandchildren. A professional writer for many years now, Allison's poetry is sold as framed prints by Home Interiors and Gifts. Readers can find more of Allison's intimate and heartwarming poetry at *www.allisonsheart.com*.

Candy Dugger Thanks to this lady for keeping me on focus so much, what a joy! Her quick typing was a major blessing and without her this book would still be in the formatting stages. She's a great friend and worker. This is the beginning of just another fun adventure with a great team. Thanks for all your hard work and long hours. I am blessed!

Brenda Ball communicates with innocent words of wisdom the writings that will touch your heart and soul. First published at age 23, Brenda has been blessed with a great literary talent. Professionally, her career choices have been enriched by her ability to communicate with the written word. Now living in Castlewood, Virginia (a small, rural town nestled beautifully at the foothills of the Blue Ridge Mountains) with her husband, Butch, and her youngest sons, she loves being a stay-at-home wife/mother/poet/writer.

Over the years writing has become a passion for Brenda; she believes that, *Poetry is God's way of writing upon one's soul."* The author of over two-hundred poems, Brenda is presently working on her first novel. She is also developing a new series of children's books based on the antics of her five year old granddaughter. Readers can look forward to seeing more of her work in upcoming publications.

Sue Dreamer, discovered at a young age she was overflowing imagination and creativity. She loved to draw, sew, and work on crafts with her mother. This passion to illustrate has driven Sue to achieve success she enjoys today, engaging for two decades, a loyal following of fans who seek out her unique style of artwork. More of her work can be found at: *www.suedreamer.com.*

Joe Thompson has been writing poems and songs for kids since he was a kid himself. But when his children, Martin and Leslie, were born, the process took on a new meaning.

By day, Joe is a high school Art teacher. By night, he is a jack of all trades. Besides poetry, Joe also writes and performs original music; he has two family oriented CDs that are available on the internet. He also acts in and directs plays. All while embracing life and enjoying his family. Many of his poems, skits, and songs are online at his website: *www.imaginesongs.com.*

Dorothea K. Barwick was born in New York in 1939. She moved to South Carolina in 1960. Both she and her husband had been previously married, and each brought three children into the marriage. They also adopted a son, have ten grandchildren. Beth Anne is their precious Special Needs child. She was born with Rett Syndrome which is a disorder causing diabetes, seizures, and her inability to walk or talk. They have also been blessed by the love of three great-grandchildren. Dorothea feels that sharing her poetry is her way of honoring God and thanking Him for the blessings he has bestowed upon her.

Dorothea is the owner of Handmaiden Creations in Hopkins, SC. More of her work can be found at: *www.handmaidencreations@sc.rr.com.*

Barbara Cox, native to Phoenix, AZ, is the only child of Henry and Geraldine Butler. Barbara found her love for writing when she took a journalism class in high school. Later, in her forties, she began writing poetry after the birth of her oldest grandson. She is the author of many articles and poems, and has been published by local newspapers and magazines.

Barbara credits her wealth of love and inspiration to her children, grandchildren, dear friends, and God. The intense connection she feels with the subject matter derives from their love. More of her inspiring works can be found at: *www.geocities.com/barbcox2u/*

The author wishes to thank DeskGallery: Clip-Art Library for their invaluable collection of clip art. Our special thanks to Zedcor, Inc. for granting permission to use this fabulous product in this new book.

Dover Publications Thanks for the spectacular collection of Art Nouveau designs. This collection made possible the visual expression of the artists' written word. It proved to be an invaluable resource in Celebrating Kids.

Lottie Ann Knox has been giving the majority of her poetry as gifts. She was born in Royston, Georgia on May 31, 1948. Using her God-given talent, she has written poetry all of her life. Her writings are inspired by her love for the Lord. Her many hobbies include: making and decorating cakes, cross-stitch, crochet, and genealogical research. Lottie is a Christian member of The Church of Jesus Christ of Latter Day Saints who now lives in the panhandle of Florida. Readers can find more of her poetry at *www.poetry.com* and *www.poetspassion.com*.

Laurie Connable has a passion for God, people of all ages, and the gift of creativity. Inspired by her childhood in Hawaii and her children, she wrote, recorded, published, and performed "I Love Life", "I love Life 2" and "I'm A New Creation". She currently resides in San Diego, CA. Working as an illustrator, Laurie travels widely and looks forward to sharing her music and poetry with her grandchildren. *www.ilovelife.com*

Crystal Jones and **Camilla Smith** have been an encouragement and a source of strength and prayer throughout this journey of writing and pubishing. I am so blessed to call them friend. Check out Camilla's work at her website *www.platinumheart.com*

Linda LaTourelle has been writing since her childhood. In writing this book she hopes to enable others to see how all children are precious to the Lord. In her own words, "My prayer is that through scripture, the writings of others' and my own writing, this book will be a blessing to all who read it. Children are the light of life!"

Triumphant over personal adversities, it is because of her children and their blessed relationship that she will succeed. Look for more wonderful and insightful books to come from Linda.

Be looking for
these new books
coming soon
by
Linda LaTourelle
& Friends

The Ultimate Guide
to Celebrating Kids
Volume 2

The Ultimate Guide
to Tweens & Teens

The Ultimate Guide
to Family & Friends

The Ultimate Guide
To the Perfect Card
(Bigger and Better)

& MORE surprises coming...

BLUE GRASS
Publishing
Mayfield, KY

• • • • • • • • • • • • • • • • • •

Need another book?

Are you looking at your friend's book right now?
**Order your own copy below
or go to our website at:**
www.theultimateword.com
Send us an E-mail:
service@theultimateword.com

....

MAIL ORDER FORM

Please send _____ copy/s of:
The ULTIMATE Guide to Celebrating Kids

Name: _____

Address: _____

City: _____State_____Zip: _____

E-mail: _____Phone: _____

*Please include $19.95 plus $2.95 s/h (per book)
(KY add 6% tax)*

Blue Grass Publishing
PO Box 634
Mayfield, KY 42066
Tel. 270.251.3600

....

If you're looking for a gift that will be
well-loved and used regularly order now...
The ULTIMATE Guide to Celebrating Kids
Available at your local scrapbook retailer, too.
Visit our website for **MORE** fun books & store info

www.theultimateword.com

Favorite Quotes

No other blessing is so sweet as the heart of a child

Favorite Quotes

Hug a child and feel your heart soar

Blessings abound in the presence of a child

A child's love is the
kind that makes
heaven touch earth

More surprises coming soon
to truly delight you!
visit us at:
www.theultimateword.com
(270) 251.3600